Natural Law and Human Rights

CATHOLIC IDEAS FOR A SECULAR WORLD

O. Carter Snead, series editor

DE NICOLA CENTER
for ETHICS AND CULTURE

Under the sponsorship of the de Nicola Center for Ethics and Culture at the University of Notre Dame, the purpose of this interdisciplinary series is to feature authors from around the world who will expand the influence of Catholic thought on the most important conversations in academia and the public square. The series is "Catholic" in the sense that the books will emphasize and engage the enduring themes of human dignity and flourishing, the common good, truth, beauty, justice, and freedom in ways that reflect and deepen principles affirmed by the Catholic Church for millennia. It is not limited to Catholic authors or even works that explicitly take Catholic principles as a point of departure. Its books are intended to demonstrate the diversity and enhance the relevance of these enduring themes and principles in numerous subjects, ranging from the arts and humanities to the sciences.

NATURAL LAW AND HUMAN RIGHTS

Toward a Recovery of Practical Reason

PIERRE MANENT

Translated by Ralph C. Hancock
Foreword by Daniel J. Mahoney

University of Notre Dame Press
Notre Dame, Indiana

University of Notre Dame Press
Notre Dame, Indiana 46556
undpress.nd.edu

All Rights Reserved

Copyright © 2020 by University of Notre Dame

Published in the United States of America

Library of Congress Control Number: 2019054504

ISBN-13: 978-0-268-10721-5 (Hardback)

ISBN-13: 978-0-268-10722-2 (Paperback)

ISBN: 978-0-268-10724-6 (WebPDF)

ISBN: 978-0-268-10723-9 (Epub)

CONTENTS

FOREWORD

Natural Law and the Restoration of Practical Reason

Daniel J. Mahoney

The French political philosopher Pierre Manent has explored the "theological-political problem" in a series of works culminating in his 2015 book *Situation de la France*, which appeared a year later in English as *Beyond Radical Secularism*. In this study, Manent expresses reservations about militant secularism, affirms the "Christian mark" of France and other European nations, and sympathetically treats the contribution Jews have made to European civilization. Manent makes the challenging argument that the successful absorption of French and European Muslims depends on European democracy maintaining its civilizational soul. Muslims must not enter an empty space—a "wasteland"—where they would be free to affirm the *umma* instead of becoming loyal citizens of the countries in which they now live. Further, Manent reflects on "political action and the common good," contending that the human good is not unsupported, and that we do not live in a merely arbitrary world; political action, he maintains, should be guided and informed by the old cardinal virtues: courage, prudence, temperance, and justice. As Manent put it in a 2014 essay,

"Knowledge and Politics" (his farewell address at the *École des Hautes Études en Sciences Sociales*), "If we have the right to speak of humanity as a species sharing a common nature, this is because of this pattern of practical virtues, by which we recognize a courageous and just person in the human being born in the most distant and apparently different latitude."

Manent published another book in March 2018, *La loi naturelle et les droits de l'homme*, which deepens the considerations of *Beyond Radical Secularism* and challenges the humanitarian civil religion that has dominated European intellectual circles since at least May 1968. The new book occasioned lively discussions in France and is now appearing in English from University of Notre Dame Press under the title *Natural Law and Human Rights: Toward a Recovery of Practical Reason*. In six chapters developed from the prestigious Étienne Gilson lectures at the Institut Catholique de Paris (and in a related appendix on Saint Thomas and the recovery of the intelligibility of law), Manent reflects on the steady displacement of the natural law by the modern conception of human rights. He questions the widely shared notion of human rights that radically separates them, legitimate as they are in their own sphere, from the ends of human freedom. Manent rejects the fiction of human "autonomy"—a groundless freedom, without reasons or purposes, to make our way in the world. Nor is he a partisan of "heteronomy," where acting human beings take their direction from the will of others. Such categories are far too abstract; they tell us nothing about the "rules" inherent in human action itself. Those rules become clear as we act conscientiously in the world, trying to do justice to the sense of right and wrong that defines us as human beings. Starting from moral and political philosophy, from an eminently "practical world," and not from theology or metaphysics (although Manent is in no way opposed to metaphysical reflection), Manent sets out to recover natural law as the key instrument vivifying free will, human choice, and moral and political action.

La loi naturelle et les droits de l'homme confronts the prejudices, or dogmas, of those who have repudiated the classical and (especially) Christian notion of "liberty under law." Manent denies that we can generate obligations from a condition of what Locke, Hobbes, and

Rousseau call the "state of nature," where human beings are absolutely free, with no obligations to others. Manent's book is an exercise in defending liberty under law, in both the Christian and the political senses of the term. In his view, our ever-more-imperial affirmation of human rights needs to be reintegrated into what he calls an "archic" understanding of human and political existence, where law and obligation are inherent in liberty and meaningful human action. Otherwise, we are bound to act thoughtlessly, in an increasingly arbitrary or willful manner. Manent aims to restore the grammar of moral and political action, and thus the possibility of an authentically *political* order, one fully compatible with liberty rightly understood.

In the opening chapter, "Why Natural Law Matters," Manent highlights the incoherence of a rights project that combines apolitical universalism and a thoughtless cultural relativism. Commentators such as Olivier Roy condemn, for instance, Christian opposition to LGBT rights but welcome, in the name of cultural tolerance, a far more vociferous opposition to them from European Muslims. The West is always judged severely, in this way of thinking, while the "Other" gets a free pass. As Manent demonstrates, politically and juridically imposed same-sex marriage was not a modest change in the law to make marriage more "inclusive" but a systematic assault on the idea of a normative human nature. It changed the very nature of marriage, undercutting its natural foundations. Marriage—"the crucial institution of a human world organized according to natural law"— no longer acknowledges the complementarity of the sexes or the natural foundations of family life. Transgenderism continues this rejection of the very idea of human nature and an authoritative natural moral law, where sex is radically separated from "gender." That is surely worthy of reflection and debate before gender ideology becomes a tyrannical orthodoxy beyond dispute.

Manent's latest work is above all an effort to reactivate the perspective of the citizen or religious believer who truly acts in the human world. In the second chapter, "Counsels of Fear," Manent challenges a widely held belief that Machiavelli and other early modern political philosophers liberated a salutary practical perspective against the one-sidedly contemplative emphases of classical and

Christian thought. This is to turn everything upside down, Manent believes. It was the classics and the Christians who defended "reflective choice" and "free will," the preconditions of all meaningful action. By contrast, Machiavelli, writing at the dawn of modernity, substituted a *theoretical* perspective on action that eclipsed the agent's point of view. The rationale for this assault on practical action shows up most revealingly in chapters 15 and 18 of Machiavelli's *The Prince*. Machiavelli could not abide the gap between "what is done" and "what should be done." This distinction, so central to practical action and reflective choice, becomes, for Machiavelli, an unbridgeable chasm that confuses and enervates human beings. The chasm, he contended, must be closed once and for all. Machiavelli counsels subduing *fortuna*, but he has no place for reflective choice or moral prudence—the crown of the virtues, according to Aristotle.

Machiavelli succumbs to, and instills in his readers, an excessive desire for clarity, Manent writes, a desire that ends up denying that true action is always and everywhere subordinate to law. Machiavelli's evocative rhetoric and audacious theorizing helped decisively to undermine the gap between what people do and what they ought to do, which is the horizon and precondition of all reasonable choice. In his assault on "imaginary principalities" (such as the perennial notion of natural law) in chapter 15 of *The Prince*, he frees "virtuosos of action," daring revolutionaries of a new type, from adherence to the natural law. "Necessity," a willingness to move back and forth between good and evil with an exhilarating alacrity, and immoral daring, become the trademark of those "princes" freed from the constraints of the moral law. They feign respect for that law—see chapter 18 of *The Prince*—but have no real place for it in their souls.

It is in this context, Manent observes, that Machiavelli sets out to promote the "erasure or eradication of conscience." By "conscience," Manent does not mean its pale modern substitute: subjective arbitrariness or personal whim. He has in mind that firm interior guide, "brought to light only in a Christian context," which allowed an acting human being to discern between good and evil, better and worse, in the context of moral and political action. Conscience, however imperfectly, allows us to see our actions as a just God sees them.

This is the law "written in the human heart" of which Saint Paul spoke. But conscience is knowable through human experience and self-knowledge and does not depend for its recognition on revelation alone. Manent affirms that "the notion of conscience supports and complements the Aristotelian analysis of practical life and reflective choice so well that the two elements prove to be inseparable" (see n. 21 in ch. 2). Without the notion of conscience, practical reason is bereft and loses its foothold in the human world. By repudiating conscience, by deciding to bury it once and for all, Machiavelli gave birth to a wholly abstract perspective on moral and political life. A new conception of human freedom, ever tethered to necessity, would expel conscience and practical reason from human and political life. For Manent, Aristotle and Christianity, reflective choice and free will and conscience, stand or fall together. They are the indispensable ground of practical life and practical reason.

Machiavellian modernity nevertheless finds powerful reinforcement in the Protestant Reformation's paradoxical undermining of "liberty under law." For Martin Luther, there was no free will; salvation owes everything to grace. For the "acting Christian," the Christian *agent*, the pre-Reformation Christian, who takes his bearings from conscience and the natural law, there is no certitude about salvation, though "good works" show human freedom, aided by grace, responding the call of the law; there is no possibility of escaping the tensions between what we are (imperfect sinners) and what we ought to do and become.

The acting Christian does his best to live virtuously in light of the cardinal and theological virtues. Manent is a partisan of this acting Christian, who remains subject to natural law and the requirements of conscience and who does not appeal to a "Christian liberty" contemptuous of natural law. Against Machiavelli and Luther, Manent defends the sempiternal requirements of liberty under law. A scholar following in Manent's footsteps might feel compelled to develop his suggestive argument that Aristotelian reflective choice (the deliberation and prudence of books 3 and 6 of the *Nicomachean Ethics*) vitally depends on conscience. Reflective choice and the moral conscience unearthed in a Christian context are the twin pillars of a practical philosophy that respects the "archic" character of human freedom. Human freedom, that is, can never be truly groundless. True freedom is never arbitrary, never simply willful. Action is always accompanied by rules, by ends, purposes, and finalities, which provide guidance for the exercise of human choice. Without natural law, choice is utterly arbitrary and self-destructive, an example of the will willing itself. Reasonable action becomes impossible, and the moral and political agent is left bereft in the world.

The central chapters of *Natural Law and Human Rights* address the curious relationship between the modern state of Machiavellian and, later, Hobbesian origin (which protects ever-expanding rights but ignores the *reasons* at the heart of political disputation) and modern man's singular inability either to command or to obey, in the fulsome sense of those words. Manent provocatively advances the claim that the "empire" of the modern state, representative or not, has witnessed a growing erosion of human capacity for action. The state undermines authentic statesmanship and citizenship, legitimate authority (which is never simply willful or authoritarian), and obedience to a political community that governs wisely and well. This paralysis of command and obedience is rooted in the "irreparable error" of modern natural right, which is to think that it is "possible to produce the command starting from a condition of noncommand"— from that illusion that is interchangeably called "natural freedom" or "the state of nature."

Moreover, as Manent makes clear in chapter 4, while there "is no human condition without command," the practical world, the world of reflective choice and deliberation, "is never given over essentially to the arbitrary commands of gods or of human beings." "The human agent," Manent observes, "cannot engage in action without entering to some degree into its reasons." Arbitrary command is thus a contradiction in terms. Once again, we live in an "archic" world—one interwoven with rules and purposes intrinsic to thoughtful action. Law, both positive and natural, is inseparable from our liberty.

Manent does not seek to bury human rights and the regime of modern liberty, as a superficial reading of this book might suggest. He writes, here and elsewhere, with some admiration for the ability of early modern republics to give rise to "common action," to a prodigious redefinition of the common, or the commonweal. As Manent had already argued in *Les métamorphoses de la cité* (2010; translated as *Metamorphoses of the City*, 2013), for a time, modernity unleashed a remarkable energy and put forward new and impressive visions of republican civic life. It gave rise to a truly dynamic, self-confident political and social order. But sometime in the 1960s, we reached a "point of inflection," where the endless extension of rights began to rob essential institutions of their meaning and substance. In Western Europe, the Catholic Church, the liberal university, and the self-governing nation "had to confront a radical contestation of their proper legitimacy and their internal meaning." Not only were rules relaxed, but the very telos of authoritative institutions was denied in favor of the radical autonomy of the individual, more and more disconnected from the political, social, and moral contents of human individuality.

Today, church leaders and activists alike defend the right of any human being to become a citizen of any country that that person chooses. Through a failure to interrogate itself about its own political and cultural preconditions, the regime of indiscriminate rights ceases to support a meaningful political common good. It has no boundaries in principle and can make no substantive demands on those living within its territory. It depoliticizes democracy and begins actively to war on the ends and purposes that inform a freedom worthy of the name. Rights become the alpha and the omega of the human and political world, and those who make ever-more-insistent rights claims will tolerate no dissent.

Manent does not hide the fact that theoretical liberalism—the liberalism of Hobbes, Spinoza, and Bayle—resolutely opposed both the Greek conception of reflective choice and the Christian notions of free will and conscience. Modern materialism and determinism cannot support the common action and moral responsibility that are necessary foundations of human liberty, even under modern circumstances. A true liberalism needs reflective choice, a commonsense affirmation of free will, and a nonsubjectivist notion of conscience to defend the dignity of the acting human being and to establish the space and preconditions of politics, understood as a realm of thoughtful—and common—action.

Thomas Hobbes constructed the edifice of the liberal state and society on the "fear of violent death." But as Manent rightly observes in chapter 5 ("The Individual and the Agent"), there is something terribly debilitating about treating death as an "extrinsic accident," with an overweening place in our awareness. For the acting human being and the acting Christian, death cannot be the central concern of human existence. All people fear death, and we should not exaggerate the courage of most in this regard. But the acting person, though "naturally afraid of death," Manent explains, does not do everything and anything to avoid it. He is concerned above all with doing the right thing, with seeking the right action and respecting the rules and priorities inherent in a serious human life. We are sometimes commanded, not by arbitrary authority but by the authority of what is right and good, to put ourselves at some mortal risk. Self-preservation can never be the great desideratum for a human being guided by reflective choice and a conscience that honors truth and virtue. The great task of human beings is living well, and not preserving this-worldly existence indefinitely. On this Plato, Aristotle, Seneca, and Saint Paul would surely agree.

Manent exposes the growing toleration of the liberal state for taking the lives of the sick and the infirm. Treating death as an external obstacle leads some to claim, paradoxically, that they can make authoritative judgments on the "subjective sentiment" of a sick or infirm person. The old and always authoritative verity—"thou shall not kill"—is thrown to the wind by the same people who treat the death penalty as an absolute abomination. Modern liberty, in its most extreme theoretical articulations and applications, has replaced liberty under law with a one-sided preoccupation with death as the *summum malum*. We are clearly in unchartered territory. Only by accepting death as an essential part of life, and not as an "extrinsic accident" to be overcome, can we restore respect for life at every stage of human existence.

Manent's book concludes with an account in chapter 6 of "natural law and human motives," which has already appeared in English in modified form in the journal *Modern Age*. Building on Aristotle, Manent shows how no human being can act without deferring to the three great human motives: the pleasant, the useful, and the honorable (or the just and noble). These are the "objective components of human nature." Cultures and civilizations vary, and humanity consists, in Plato's words, of a "coat of many colors." But because human beings share three great constitutive motives, we are obliged to judge others and ourselves (one might add that we are equally obliged to find the appropriate means to those fixed and enduring ends of human virtue which are courage, justice, temperance, and prudence). Yet we are not prisoners of our motives, since moral virtue demands that we conjugate them in a way that does justice to a balanced and virtuous life. Our human nature is completed by the exercise of the cardinal and theological virtues that allow us to live well as human beings. As Manent explains, the jihadist or Islamist terrorist who kills in the name of a mutilated conception of religion is nothing more than a criminal who has degraded a noble conception of justice. We must judge him for the criminal we would be, too, if we, too, turned justice into an excuse for murder.

In Manent's words, "The very notion of natural law presupposes or implies that we have the ability to judge human conduct according to criteria that are clear, stable, and largely if not universally shared." Human diversity, especially in the cultural realm, is fully compatible with rules of justice comprehensible to human beings as human beings. The principal motives of human action—the pleasant, the useful, and the noble—define the criteria for moral judgment and political action. Manent is not deterred by the "fact-value distinction" or the "naturalistic fallacy" beloved by social scientists and some academic philosophers. One can indeed "locate a valid rule of action on the basis of a description" of human motives, since our motives unfold within an "archic" world. There is not an unbridgeable gap but rather a "gentle slope" connecting the "is" and the "ought," between what we are and what we ought to be. Such is the foundational truth of the human world.

We have seen that Manent refuses to identify the noble with those who have open contempt for the moral law, such as jihadist terrorists. He expands his analysis to discuss communism and a conception of marriage compatible with the natural law. A student of the great anti-communist French thinker Raymond Aron, Manent argues that the communist regime was in violation of the natural law. He speaks of it as "sinister" and acknowledges its terrible crimes. But he thinks discussion of communism has been inordinately preoccupied with the question of communist "ideals," which lead too many people away from confronting its dark reality. Manent points to another path of judgment, narrower and thus incomplete but nonetheless "rigorously correct" on its own terms: communist regimes so frustrated the "fundamental" wellsprings of human life (think of collectivization, periodic famines in all major communist countries, and systematic consumer shortages) that the regime could never honor basic human needs. It could not do justice to the elementary place of the useful and pleasant in any decent life.

Manent is not unaware of—or silent about—the gulags, torture, and the Big Lie. Elsewhere, he has commented authoritatively on all the sinister features of the ideological regime. Manent perfectly understands the "essential imperfections," as Raymond Aron called them, of communist totalitarianism. His argument about the incompatibility of communism with the natural law is partial but convincing on its own terms.

Manent argues, as well, that marriage understood in terms of the natural law must give "appropriate place to the three motives"; it cannot be reduced to pleasure-seeking or "changing feelings." His argument is not explicitly biblical or Catholic, but maintains that marriage cannot be adequately understood within the framework of some alleged human autonomy that justifies jettisoning one's broader moral responsibilities. The natural law is a starting place for judgment: the cultivation of human nobility can help develop virtuous human conduct in an even richer and more humanizing way. Nobility can enlarge our sense of obligation and can put the useful and the pleasant in their proper place, without denying their centrality in a balanced and morally serious life.

As Manent stresses, prudence plays a key role in all of these deliberations. That is one reason why he is so skeptical of replacing natural-law reasoning with an ever-expanding list of human rights. He decries the "tyranny of the explicit" in regard to rights and rights claims. When rights become too numerous and explicit, they introduce debilitating conflict into civil society. Moral agents need to leave a substantial place for prudence and for genuinely moral and political deliberation. Excessive "rights talk" corrupts moral reasoning and civic debate by making thoughtful compromise much less likely.

An appendix to the book, "Recovering Law's Intelligence," originally appeared in the *Revue Thomiste* in 2014. It appears here with Pierre Manent's permission. In multiple ways, it clarifies the intentions of Manent's Gilson lectures. This chapter boldly argues that Thomas Aquinas, the greatest doctor of the church, is "the author who can best help . . . Christians as well as non-Christians" alike to confront and overcome "the loss of law's meaning." This return to Saint Thomas cannot, however, be direct or unmediated: "We cannot proceed as if nothing had happened for seven or eight centuries." During those centuries, the Western world found itself under the tutelage of another Thomas, Thomas Hobbes, who reduced human motives to but one, the desire for power that "ceaseth only in death." With Thomas Aquinas's (and Aristotle's) help, Manent recovers the rich and ample heterogeneity of human motives. Rather than being prisoners of the language of rights, those who return to the wisdom of Aristotle and Thomas (without in any way rejecting the immense practical benefits of the liberal democratic order) can recover the precious idea of an enduring human bond that makes possible "common action" and "commanding law." What commands is not arbitrary will but an "active political reason" that recognizes citizens and human beings as agents and persons and not as subjects of various determinisms, on the one hand, or the "spontaneous order" of the market, on the other. When Christians and citizens act politically, when they exercise the great virtue of prudence, they participate "in Providence," by providing for "ourselves and others" (see question 91 of Thomas's *Treatise on Law* as discussed and highlighted by Manent in the appendix). Eternal law has a necessary place for natural law, for the exercise of free will and "reflective choice." Saint Thomas thus allows us to understand the honored place of natural and human law in a world where freedom and responsibility are grounded in the very order of things. Manent once again affirms the primacy of the Good, the fact that the goods of life are not without natural or divine support. With impressive learning, Manent points us once again to the heterogeneous motives of the human soul and to the humanizing ends and purposes that inform our freedom. In this deep, concise, and instructive book, he shows us the way toward rejuvenating both moral and political judgment and the broader moral foundations of the modern republic. His book is a preeminent example of reflection at the service of truth—and common life.

TRANSLATOR'S INTRODUCTION

Ralph C. Hancock

Those who know Pierre Manent only by reputation as a conservative Catholic political philosopher will think they know the thrust of this book from its title: natural rights are the problem, and natural law is the solution. This formula is not exactly wrong, but it certainly risks missing the whole point—the profoundly original and challenging point—of this book.

The doctrine of natural rights, which has necessarily evolved into the doctrine of human rights, is certainly the problem. Indeed the problem is precisely that the idea or project of *natural* rights, as understood in the modern tradition of political philosophy, and most eminently and symptomatically by Thomas Hobbes, slides irresistibly into the assertion of *human* rights. The original appeal to a standard of nature dissolves into sheer human assertion. As Manent shows, this dissolution is inherent in the modern project, because the "nature" to which Hobbes and his followers appeal, nature as the radically individuated biological being, ultimately reduces to the individual's power-claim.

In the first of six chapters, Manent deftly exposes the bankruptcy of modern natural/human rights. The human rights ideology is at once universalist and relativist; it promises both to liberate the person from his physical, sexual nature and to justify him on the basis of his natural or irresistible desires or "orientation." At bottom this ideology's only coherence is purely negative; it only knows what it is against: in the name of equality (the equality of a being defined only by the right to define and to redefine himself, or herself, or itself), "human rights" wages endless war against common sense, against what is best and richest in the spontaneous expression of our natures, against (as Manent wrote already in *Tocqueville and the Nature of Democracy*) "all that has human form." Manent bravely suggests, in fact, that the successful campaign for the recognition of homosexuality in the form of "marriage for all" must be understood as a fundamentally metaphysical demand, the demand that everyone renounce natural law, that no one recognize a norm or objective that is not the assertion of a pure human will.

In the second chapter, Manent begins to point to an alternative to the moral desert of subjective rights by sketching the character and genesis of the modern project. The modern viewpoint is at once the perspective of the subject's unbounded power and that of a theoretical observer in absolute possession of his object. The triumph of willfulness is at the same time the ascendency of theory; our current practical impasse is the result of a "hypertrophy of theory." Did theory's monstrous overgrowth result from the influence of the new naturalistic physics over our understanding of the human world? Manent turns the tables on this conventional view of the history of ideas and proposes instead that the rise of theory was irresistible because the character of practice had already been obscured by Europe's political and religious circumstances. Hobbes was not wrong to complain that the European rivalry between church and state as ultimate powers caused Western man to "see double" and crippled our capacities for action. Machiavelli's and Luther's apparently opposite responses to this disabling double vision have proved to be mutually reinforcing.

To diagnose the modern response to the medieval double vision Manent begins to unveil his subtle and penetrating understanding of the very structure of human action. There is a tension or a "gap" inherent in human action. Christianity did not invent this gap, but it exaggerated it and brought it to light. It is all too human to conceive of an "imaginary republic" (Machiavelli) as the culmination of good action, which is always action in view of the common good. All human beings always fall short of consistently acting in view of a higher good; our deeds inevitably fall short of our speech. This is the natural gap. Christianity absolutized this gap by conceiving of the common good as perfectly realized only in a city of God understood to be so purely common (selfless) and so purely good (perfectly satisfying) that it was utterly beyond attainment by man's natural powers. Machiavelli and Luther were so affected by the intolerable tension of this infinite gap that they proposed to close it definitively, either by replacing normative law with fear (Machiavelli) or by reducing the good, or salvation, to the subjective act of faith (Luther). In both cases the gap inherent in action was suppressed, and human action was deprived of any higher horizon. Thus Machiavellian fear proved to be the effectual truth of radical Protestant faith.

The problem of the gap inherent in practice, as interpreted first in classical and then in Christian thought, bears closer examination. The reader will find that Manent is content to be suggestive and not fully explicit on the "most delicate point" of the role of Christianity in what one might call the rise and fall of the humanizing gap. In portraying the relationship of classical philosophy to Christian theology, Manent is attentive both to a fundamental continuity (distilled in the Christian notion of "conscience") and a momentous rupture occasioned by the infinite expansion of the gap between human means and divine end; he does not offer any obvious reconciliation of these two interpretive stances. To understand the bearing of Manent's delicate discussion and how it prepares his outline of a positive new teaching of the natural law in this book's last chapter, one might consult Manent's essay "Knowledge and Politics" (included as an appendix to *Seeing Things Politically*).[1] Here Manent defends a teaching of Aristotle's that many have found perplexing—that is, the idea that deliberation and choice concern means and not ends. The end, in a decisively practical way, always remains bound up with the means. In defending Aristotle's focus on means, Manent may be said to forswear all attempts, philosophical or theological, finally to resolve the gap between the practical, virtuous means and some philosophical or theological end.

> One can say, if one insists, that value is the purpose of action, but this is to presuppose that "value" can exist as simply posited, that it can exist independently of the means sought through deliberation. Value is the end without means, and thus it is not even an end, but at most a wish. It is the lovely but confused image of a possible action, which amounts to little unless deliberation concerning means has been set in motion. Since value is subject to the manifold of representation, the variety of values is infinite, whereas the number of actual motives of action, as we have emphasized, is actually quite limited. And since the political order is based on ongoing deliberation and action, without which it would immediately cease to be, it consists in the ceaseless setting to work of actual motives for action according to the pattern of the cardinal virtues.[2]

Manent returns explicitly to "The Christian Question" in a section of the third chapter, which I will leave to the reader to explore. He then shows how Thomas Hobbes's "moralized fear" responded to this question and effectively theorized and universalized the Machiavellian strategy of collapsing the natural gap of means and ends in human action. With Hobbes the hypertrophy of theory, the claimed superiority of the power of thinking over the matter of thought, and in particular over the natural meaning of human action, becomes fully evident. The immediate practical manifestation of this inhuman theory is the unintelligible sovereign state; its more remote consequence is the elusive but pervasive authority of global exchange and technology. Finally the modern project drives toward its soulless beginning: "At the end of its course the modern state produces a social state that asymptomatically approaches the state of nature as presupposed in its construction."

Chapters 4 and 5 further develop Manent's penetrating account of the inherent character of action, which has been obscured and all but suppressed by the collusion between the "ideal" of individual autonomy, which in fact reduces the human person to the brute assertion of a *conatus*,[3] and the abstract, end-less state that hides its governing power behind the function of guarantor of the asserted "rights" of this blind and mute *conatus*. Manent's brilliantly original account of action hovers delicately between poles that one might name voluntarism and rational teleology. On the one hand, action is necessarily, inherently, "archic": action commands, it initiates, it rules. Action is active, one might almost say creative; it is in no way reducible to the straightforward application of a rule or preexisting template. Action involves an irreducible element of personal response, a singular ruling response to a singular practical opportunity. "Thus there are only commands and the act of commanding, *in this world or in the other*, because action and the human agent are naturally and necessarily under the rule of action" (emphasis added).

On the other hand, action is never arbitrary or purely "creative"; action always asserts a reason for its rule: "Action and the human agent are naturally and necessarily under the rule of action. . . . The practical world is never given over essentially to the arbitrary commands *of gods or of men*, because along with action come the reasons for action, and because the human agent cannot engage in action without entering to some degree into its reasons" (emphasis added).

Human action and practical reason thus naturally fuse commanding (the "archic," ruling/initiating) with reasoning: virtuous action accomplishes reason in a commanding act.[4] Thus Manent proposes precisely not to resolve but to recover and respect the gap inherent in action, a kind of virtuous circle that links human means and divine end. However great we conceive the gap between God and human beings to be, it cannot finally displace the humanizing gap, the insuperable circle, between end and means. Not even the ever-looming fact of mortality, ground zero for the deconstruction of common, "inauthentic" human being-in-the-world in both atheistic and transcendent discourses of absolute otherness, can distract or discourage Pierre Manent from his faithful attachment to the practical ground of human meaning:

If the agent, the acting human being, despite his fear, his great fear of death, does not, unlike the free individual, spend every effort to avoid or avert death, this is precisely because he is an agent, an acting human being, and as such obeys his nature and the logic of action. . . . As an agent he is in search of the right action, which has its rules and priorities, and which thus may include and even command acting in a way that implies mortal risk. It is not that he looks at death without blinking; it is that in acting he looks first at the rule of action, and death or the fear of death cannot be the main thing on his mind.

Keeping in mind Manent's critique of theoretical hypertrophy and his resolute respect for the meaning inherent in practice, the reader will be prepared to appreciate the audacious modesty of his outline of a positive account of natural law in his final chapter. Manent's natural law does not begin with some "organic" or "communitarian" vision of a "certain idea of nature" as the objective synthesis of all desirable norms. Rather, the author posits natural law as free action in view of the three basic kinds of motives available to human beings, motives that recall Aristotle's three kinds of friendship: the pleasant, the useful, and the "honnête" (this last resonating with both the "noble" and the "just"). If the simple acknowledgment of the pleasant and the useful seems to evoke a rather "low but solid" ground of natural law, then the latitude, the judgment, the agency inherent in the determination of the noble point to the law's participation in the highest goods. "Among all beings . . . the rational creature is subject to divine Providence in a more excellent way, in that it is itself made a participant in this Providence, by providing for itself and for others."[5]

The ground of Pierre Manent's approach to natural law is his confidence in the perspective of the agent. The author's respectful attention to the meaning inherent in action itself provides him the key to "recovering law's intelligence," and thus to appreciating the goodness of human action as it points beyond practical virtue to a divine goodness that, like the goodness of action itself, must always exceed the grasp of theoretical or theological reasoning. The excessive meaning of the practical and the excessive meaning of the divine cannot fail to color each other. (See emphases above.) It is confidence in this goodness that carries Manent as an agent as well as a thinker beyond the delicate historical question of the philosophical and theological genesis of the modern hypertrophy of theory to embrace the possibility of an unprecedented recovery of natural law. Our situation as practical rational beings is no longer defined by the contest between philosophy and theology, but instead by the good that is at work in both, but that both, as they opposed each other in our Western history, tended to obscure. As he explains in the appendix to this volume: "The problem is no longer to define the border and to order relations among two institutions, one political and the other religious, both equally ambitious and proud, but to measure the content in terms of the common good of this mixed law that has defined the Christian custom of Europe over the centuries and that is rediscovering an unexpected ordering power."

The recovery of law's intelligence thus involves a respectful but firm adieu to the long Western rivalry between the two versions of theoretical hypertrophy. Stepping away from this rivalry, the author invites us to open our minds and hearts to the goods, at once practical and divine, useful and noble, that have long summoned us both to act and to pray. To choose the right means for the right reason, and in doing so to know oneself as participating in, even as contributing to, the very order of creation—this is the humble simplicity and the fearless majesty of the vision Pierre Manent begins here to propose to us.

Pierre Manent's lucid prose, which conveys a mind both master of its ideas and respectful of the intransigent realities to which these ideas give access, is always a pleasure to translate. Some of his arguments will surprise, and thus appear quite dense to the unfamiliar reader. But the reader's due attention to the argument allows this density to reveal itself as the compactness of an argument that has taken everything into account without reviewing everything.

There are always hard choices to make in a translation, and the more the translator loves the original, the harder the choices. Manent's bracing directness, which may sometimes stretch common French usage itself just a bit, does not always translate into the most familiar English idiom. Endeavoring to strike the usual translator's balance between faithfulness and idiom, I willingly confess succumbing overall to the temptations of faithfulness to the French original.

A key, intractable example is the author's use of *"commande"*— which could be rendered either "command" or "commandment." Since "commandment" suggests an exclusively religious usage in English, I have favored "command." Still, the term, already bracing in French, may sound downright harsh in English. Well, so be it: Manent's argument compels us to come to terms with the commanding side of action. And this is as it should be. (See both D. Mahoney's introductory comments above and my own here for a proper contextualization of this commanding dimension.)

The reader who will enter into Manent's idiom as I have done my best to render it in English will find a whole world of insight opened up to him or her—a world in which a recovery of "law's intelligence" is a real and blessed possibility.

I thank University of Notre Dame Press's anonymous reviewers for helpful suggestions on the translation. And I thank most especially the author, Pierre Manent, for his invaluable consultations and his friendly encouragement in this translation project.

ONE

Why Natural Law Matters

By invitation from the Étienne Gilson Chair and Dean Philippe Capelle, whom I thank for his confidence in me and for his encouragement, I have thus undertaken, without consulting my capacities, to treat a notion—natural law—that is distinguished for having been radically discredited by modern philosophy and for now being the object of unanimous contempt by enlightened opinion.[1] This opinion excludes it from public debate as supposedly archaic and because it is supposed to pose an obstacle to the recognition and implementation of human rights. It cannot be said that it is left absolutely without honor, because it is the object of scholarly, historical, and systematic studies, and certain sectors of Catholic thought continue to recur to it as a relevant or even indispensable notion for orienting ourselves in the human world.

In any case, rejected as a thing of the past or confined to a unique and singular, though venerable, tradition, it is absent from the moral and political debates in which it once played a central role. One might say without paradox that it is by its absence, or by the decree of illegitimacy under which it suffers, that it contributes today to shaping the public debate, or what takes the place of such a debate. This, then, is how I would sum up, perhaps a little cavalierly, the role assigned among us to the natural law, to the very notion or principle of natural law.

The Great Contradiction, or the Knot That Cannot Be Untied

Nevertheless, even if all that is credible and authoritative would dissuade us from taking the smallest step in the direction of the question of natural law, this question comes to us—in a form, to be sure, that is hardly recognizable—in a very public contradiction that embarrasses us more each day. What is this contradiction? It seems that, depending on the direction of our interest and of our intention, we sometimes recur without hesitation to a universal criterion that demands and obtains the adherence of anyone possessing reason, and sometimes we dismiss all thought of such a criterion and congratulate ourselves equally on this resolution. In effect, depending on whether we look "elsewhere" or "here," either we utterly reject the very idea of a universal norm, or we eagerly appeal to it. When I say "we," I have in mind the citizens of modern democracies insofar as they adhere to the idea of justice that the progress of the Enlightenment seems to have validated, the idea that finds its canonical expression in the philosophy of human rights. When I say "here," I designate a bit hastily the West as a whole, and thus, by "elsewhere" I consider what is external to the West. More precisely, "here" is the human domain where enlightened citizens—that is, citizens informed of their rights and more generally of human rights—act; "elsewhere" is the human domain where these same citizens look and where they neither live nor act regularly, not being citizens there.

Now, depending on whether we are acting or looking, whether we are citizens or observers, it seems that our mind takes on different forms, proceeding with the same confidence in opposite directions.

When we look "elsewhere," in the direction of "cultures," or "civilizations," external to us or "exotic" in the proper sense of the term, in the direction of those that have provided material of infinite diversity to the ingenious theorizing of ethnologists, and which continue to excite the curiosity of tourists, we make it a duty and a point of pride not to judge them; we flatter ourselves that we are not shocked by practices observed there that are sometimes quite shocking and that, according to us, in keeping with our guiding philosophy, find a meaning that is reasonable, or acceptable, or in any case innocent, in this ordered and coherent whole that is the "culture" under consideration. On the other hand, when we are dealing with the domain in which we act, where we are citizens, we leave no stone unturned; our reforming zeal is indefatigable and the judgment that we bring to bear on our social and moral arrangements, which in our eyes are always in some way wrong, irrational, and unacceptable, is implacable in its severity. "Elsewhere," we would blush to claim to change anything in "their ways"; "here," the disapproval of dominant opinion, the point of view that makes the rules, comes down on those who might wish to preserve something of "our ways."

"Elsewhere," we suspend judgment concerning "exotic" ways of life, since we must by all means avoid suggesting or implying in any way that our way of life might be superior to theirs; "here," we are under constant pressure to reform, and it would be unacceptable to let things be, since nothing is more urgent or more right for men and women like us than to recognize, declare, and demand our rights, all our rights, our human rights.

This divided state of mind is characteristic of the progressive posture we have adopted as the power of the West has begun to ebb. It continues to dominate public thinking even as it produces a growing malaise—since people from "elsewhere" have arrived "here" in large numbers—and as "their ways" are adopted in the space where we act rather than characterizing only the space that we observe or visit. To be sure, what we call globalization has effaced the line separating "us" from "them" and thus encouraged the extension of our criteria to the world's population as a whole. In particular, nongovernmental organizations and international institutions lead very active campaigns throughout the world for the rights of women or the rights of children, campaigns that very explicitly and even emphatically address all human beings wherever they may live. And yet the division of which I speak is not overcome; indeed it is enhanced and made still more troubling. In effect, on the one hand, we hold that human rights are a rigorously universal principle, valid for all human beings without exception; on the other, we hold that all "cultures," all ways of life, are equal and that any tendency to judge them in the full sense of the term, or any tendency that would even consider the possibility of ranking them according to some moral standard, would be a form of discrimination, and thus that any judgment in the full sense would be an attack on human equality. On the one hand, all human beings are equal; on the other, all "cultures" have a right to equal respect, even those that violate human equality—for example, as happens in many cases, by keeping women in a subordinate position. All cultures are equal because they are made up of human beings and it is human beings who give them life; if I belittle a given culture because that culture belittles women, then I belittle all the human beings that are members of that culture, and thus by my judgment I exhibit the very inequality that I had reproved and proposed to fight. It is not a rare occurrence to see the same person become indignant over the condition of women under a Muslim regime and in the same breath condemn any pejorative reflection or criticism leveled against Islam as a human community and a way of life.

Thus we recognize a universal criterion, and we proclaim its validity and render judgments according to this criterion not only "here" but "elsewhere." At the same time, we strangely restrict the scope of this judgment—we "hold ourselves back"—when there is any question of applying this judgment "elsewhere," even when this "elsewhere" is one of "people from elsewhere" who are in fact "here." We fear that, in judging the conduct of our fellow citizens of another "culture" according to the universal criterion that we claim, we might be introducing some inequality, contrary to our criterion, between "them" and "us." Not only is this criterion fully applicable only "at home," but it in effect applies only to "us," that is to say, to citizens who do not come from "elsewhere." An eminent sociologist who is a recognized specialist of Islam reproves Christians who publicly express reservations about "LGBT rights," since by this they set themselves in contradiction with "common European values," but he declares the "not necessarily liberal" Islam of "new Muslim elites" to be "compatible with our modern societies." Thus Olivier Roy explicitly reproves where Christians are concerned what he abstains from judging in Muslims.[2] It is indeed not only "at home" but also only "to us" that the criterion of human rights applies without precaution, reservation, or attenuating circumstance. Thus we wield a universal criterion of human rights, a criterion by which we pass judgment; and at the same time this criterion either commands that we judge or forbids judgment according to the point of application. The now exclusive authority of human rights simultaneously stimulates and constrains our faculty of judgment. More precisely, it stimulates our desire to judge while at the same time constraining our faculty of judgment. It is at the root of this contradictory double injunction, one that contributes in no small way to the confusion that characterizes our public debates concerning the best way to bring about social cohesion and civic friendship.

The philosophy of human rights derives its superior—and, in the end, exclusive—validity from its universality; it is "the most universal"; it is valid for each and every human being. At one and the same time, as we have just seen, this philosophy both confronts the obstacle of the diversity of human customs and yet paradoxically encourages this same diversity: the very conduct it would reprove in the name of human rights it is brought to justify, or at least to abstain from judging, since the judgment would risk leading to the conclusion that this way of life is inferior, which goes against the principle of equality that lies at the heart of the idea of human rights. How can the philosophy that demands the greatest freedom and equality among human beings be so favorable to human diversity, to the great number of ways of life that give little place to freedom and equality? I would like to make this suggestion: the almost unlimited diversity of ways of life demonstrates the almost unlimited capacity of humanity to produce itself—to produce itself *according to no rule or criterion*, whether such a rule or criterion derives its power from human nature or from human reason. Considered from this angle, the most barbarous law is seen as very remarkable evidence of this freedom, that is, of the free production by human beings of their way of life. Such a law thus calls for a special kind of admiration on our part, an admiration that refers not to the barbarous custom itself but to the plasticity of the human form of which this custom is evidence.

What we call "barbarous" indeed presents a double nature. On the one hand, it is in fact barbarous; its customs, for example, are contrary to women's rights, and we can by no means approve them; on the other hand, this very barbarism is proof that human nature, or the nature of human things, involves no principle of power or of goodness capable by itself of ordering the human world; the aberration of customs is testimony of the unpredictability or weakness of human nature as concerns any quest for the *rule* of our life. Thus, if we were to condemn the "culture" of a "barbarous" people, with no quotation marks, then we would be supposing that human nature provides a rule or an order—we would be supposing, that is, that *there is* such a thing as human nature—and at the same time that human beings can exempt themselves from it and even go directly against it. We would be supposing that barbarism results from human beings' bad use of their freedom, which is impossible because barbarism is the very form that their freedom has taken or that it has given itself. If "barbarians" were simply barbarians without quotation marks, that would mean that human beings are at once free and under a law, that they have a nature and that they do not follow it. And this would mean that the human condition is determined as freedom under law. But it is precisely this possibility above all that the philosophy of human rights intends to dismiss. By requiring that "barbarous" be put in quotes, our governing doctrine maintains a negative proposition with extensive—one might almost say infinite—implications: to be human *is not* to be free under law. The barbarism of the "barbarous" is empirical proof of the principle upon which the philosophy of rights intends to construct a new order. The unlimited plasticity of "culture" is the empirical proof of the weakness of the law in human life, the empirical proof that law, the rule of action, *is not* given along with the fact of being human, with human nature. This is the same ontological weakness of the law that the philosophy of human rights presupposes or postulates by founding the organization of the human world on the exclusive principle of human rights: since law has no intrinsic substance, we must look elsewhere for a principle of order; we must look toward human rights, in whose service the law will have to put itself, thus finding the only function consistent with its ontological weakness.

As we observe human beings who obey the rule of their culture, even the most absurd or shocking in our view, we understand that they are not free and that there is no law valid for all human beings, a law that they would be free to obey or to disobey. We understand at the same time that we can and we must practically order collective life not according to a natural law, which does not exist or in any case has no power, but by taking as our foundation a freedom to which all human beings are entitled and of which they are capable once we have renounced imposing some law on them, once we have resolved to concern ourselves exclusively with their "rights."

This division of the mind between human rights that we must put into effect and the diverse cultures that we are obliged to declare equal entails uncertainty and finally a weakness of judgment. Caught between the diversity-without-rule of cultures on the one hand and, on the other, the lawless freedom of human rights, we no longer have a solid basis for exercising practical judgment. The arrangement that brings together the affirmation of the equality of human rights and the affirmation of the equality of "cultures" or ways of life throws the faculty of judgment into an insurmountable perplexity that tends to paralyze collective action.

The State of Nature and Nature's Nakedness

Thus laws that are exotic or barbarous and our limitless freedom come together on this point: the former implicitly refute and the latter explicitly rejects the idea of a natural law, that is, the idea of freedom under law—under a law not made by freedom but that finds its support and its reason in human nature. The argument that the philosophy of human rights is constituted in opposition to the idea of a natural law, and particularly in opposition to the way this idea developed in a Christian context, finds sufficient proof in the philosophical construction that was the basis and the matrix of the doctrine of the rights of man, that is, the notion of the state of nature. The Christian or biblical idea of humanity as beginning under the law and, whether obedient or disobedient, as remaining under the law, is replaced by that of a humanity that begins in a freedom that ignores all law and that, once forced by necessity to give itself laws, will do so only under the condition and with the intention of preserving its freedom whole without law: the modern citizen, by putting himself under the law that he has produced, means to remain, according to the formula of Rousseau's *Social Contract*, "just as free as before."[3] In other words, the law henceforth has validity or legitimacy only if it aims to guarantee human rights and limits itself to this purpose.

One might argue that, although the philosophy of human rights was elaborated and refined in a Christian context in opposition to the philosophy or doctrine of natural law nourished in this context, these conditions surrounding its production—which, it is easy to show from the history of philosophy, were intensely polemical—take nothing from the intrinsic legitimacy of this philosophy. The idea of an original condition of freedom and equality in which the rights of man are rooted seems at first to offer enough consistency and meaning, enough clarity and motivation, for the citizen to be able and even obliged to forget the history of philosophy. No doubt the idea of human rights speaks to us directly and powerfully enough that we do not feel the need to inquire concerning its genesis. Still, even if we consider the notion of the state of nature to be scaffolding that is no longer needed once the edifice of rights has been constructed, a little attention to the stones of this edifice will force us to admit that we cannot speak of human rights without referring implicitly but directly and concretely to "nature." And however repugnant we may find it to consider that "nature" in any sense plays a role in the principles by which we organize the human world, we must concede that the modern doctrine of rights depends upon a specific understanding of the human being that is nothing if not "natural." The doctrine of human rights derives from a "right" that is nothing if not "natural."

In effect, the rights bearer—or, in any case, the basis of human rights—is the individual considered as distinct and separate by nature itself from other individuals, the individual as individuated by his biological nature, his nature as a living being; it is this unit of life and quantity of being that wants to continue to live and to persevere in being. Such an individual may then be enriched by all the determinations or qualities that stem from social life, but it remains that these hold together and thus constitute his individuality as a moral fact because they are all connected with this natural unit of life. It is one's *nature* as a living being, and this alone, that has the specific power to make each human being a distinct and separate individual, and so a possible subject of rights.

The expressions "biological nature" and "living being" are nevertheless imprecise or too precise. A fundamental characteristic of biological nature, of the living being, is sexual difference, which is essential to this being's reproduction, and thus to the difference of generations. But the nature that keeps human beings separate and available for equal freedom is the nature that, void of any quality that might indicate a bond and exempt from any difference of age, sex, or capacity, is strictly *the same* for all members of the species. This nature, stripped of all complexity or inner fullness, has nothing to teach us concerning the *human* being that we are—indeed it has quite little to tell us regarding ourselves as animals. This nature may *leave* us all equally free, but only for the negative reason that it bears no properly human characteristic, no *binding* characteristic. By reducing us to the most impoverished common denominator, it offers itself as a basis indifferently available for all imaginable human possibilities in their infinite variety.

Such an elemental and impoverished "nature" seems to be compatible with all possible or imaginable human "cultures." By itself it tends toward nothing that is properly human, but one can *add* to it mentally everything that reason, imagination, or human experience can observe or produce. This unit of life—sexless and ageless, with no distinct capacities—has been isolated as the basis of human rights; everything experienced by human beings can appear as a human construction devoid of foundations or natural motives. By gathering all that is natural in humanity in the separate individual—that is, in the fact of separation itself, by condensing the force and the meaning of nature into its separating power—we void the whole of the human phenomenon of all other natural determinations except for its separation into individuals, thus radically "denaturalizing" this phenomenon. Once the validity or the authority of nature has been limited to the brute fact of radical separation, what is properly human can be constructed and deconstructed as we wish, since it is devoid of the natural basis whose determining or inspiring force we should recognize. Regarding any human characteristic we can now say that it is "constructed" and that it is therefore possible or even urgent to "deconstruct" it. This approach, which transforms the human world into a Transformers toy that requires nothing but ingenuity to be understood, is founded on the mute compactness of a nature that is enclosed in the individuality of the not-even-animal-living-being. This nature involves no meaningful relations with properly human dispositions, purposes, or institutions. Its imperious silence proclaims that nothing is natural that is located beyond the separated living-individual.

We see then how different is this natural right, born by an individual so defined, from natural law. While natural law issued commands in the name of a teaching implicit in human nature, in a *tendency* of human nature to society and to knowledge, or in a natural *difference* among ages, sexes, and capacities, a tendency or difference that reason once made explicit and on the basis of which it founded its commandments and recommendations, modern natural right begins with a proposition concerning nature that reduces it to identity and separation: the bearers or bases of rights are sufficiently or even exhaustively defined by the fact that they are identical, or similar, and separate. From this identity or similarity, repeated for every separate individual we can count, it is impossible to derive any directly practical commandment or recommendation. On the other hand, one may derive—and in fact we have derived—from this identical separate self a redefinition of law whose consequences have transformed the way we understand and organize our social, political, and moral existence.

Natural inclinations or natural differences, if they exist, constitute a kind of language of nature. At the very least they engage us and, as it were, force us to speak. How many words spring from sexual differences or the differences of age! Nature understood as without inclination or difference is equality, an equality that tends toward confusion with identity or similarity, since it neither recognizes nor nourishes any differences. Thus modern natural right is disappearing before our eyes as a *natural* right, since it presents itself as an *equal* right, or simply as equality. To be sure, this equality is still considered *natural*, or according to nature, or according to a certain separate individual-living-being. It is because human rights are attached ultimately to a nature without qualities, because they promote an equality that ignores differences, that such rights are the moving force of an indefinite social, moral, and political movement that ceaselessly sets an undefinable and ever-deferred equality at odds with the inclinations and differences that human beings experience. In any case, by speaking of equality and rights rather than of natural equality, we benefit from nature's authority—albeit, once again, a most impoverished nature—while avoiding calling attention to the question of nature at the risk of having to open or reopen the debate over what is "natural." The declared rejection of all reference to a natural criterion is inseparable from this clandestine appeal to the authority of nature.

Naturalization and Denaturalization

The authority of nature has not, then, really been abolished for us where the organization of the human world is concerned. It is just that this nature, which is still at work among us, does not appear as such and, as it were, hides its power. It is a fact of similarity and of separation that neither carries with it nor promises any positive cause of action, that opens up no course of action that might be judged or evaluated qualitatively, but only an equal right to an indeterminate number of actions or rather of indeterminate "things." At the same time, since, once again, this nature reduced to a minimum continues secretly to contain the power of nature itself, it motivates and nourishes the desire for life that, even though it cannot quite be called "natural," would be experienced as such, since it conforms to the idea of nature that is at the origin of our rights. But what can be the character of a life "according to nature" when this nature bears no properly human traits? Let us at least try to conceive such a life.

Such a form of life would not understand itself as one "culture" among others, or along the lines "our ways are as good as their ways," since, as I have emphasized, this life is under the authority or the reforming norm of a certain idea of nature. Nor would it be able to understand itself as "the good society" or "the best regime," because discriminating or evaluating judgment no longer disposes of any criterion of humanity, to the point that, as we have seen, citizens have trouble passing serious judgment on things they nonetheless are inclined to condemn. This form of life would understand itself rather as the seat of an unceasing effort to authorize and encourage the individual-living-being to recompose all the significant elements of the human world in order to make them conform to the idea that he has of himself. And this presupposes that these elements or determining factors of our being-human are treated as so many artifacts that are held together by nothing but their connection with the individual-living-being. The power of nature so understood issues into the open-ended process of rendering the human world artificial. There is nothing natural but this germ of life, the separate individual-living-being, a postulate that issues into the denaturalization of all characteristics distinctive of the human being, whether it is a question of sex, age, capacities, or forms of life. Public rules as well as private conduct are required to recognize and to make it clear that none of these characteristics either results in a natural determination or can claim the authority of nature. This recomposition of the human world is presented as the concretization of human rights in their full consequences, and of course as the ultimate fulfillment of freedom, since each individual is henceforth authorized and encouraged freely to compose the bouquet of characteristics constituting the humanity he has chosen.

This free recomposition nevertheless remains ever incomplete; it always risks stalling because the preliminary effort of deconstruction encounters the resistance or the opposition of a renaturalizing tendency, a tendency represented by at least a part of social opinion and one that finds support in the subject himself whenever, summoned to *choose* his identity, he experiences the pressure or the attraction—which may be quite persuasive—of forces he has not chosen. Whether this resistance is interpreted as the weight of prejudices or as the spontaneous self-defense of human nature, the society of deconstruction-recomposition according to human rights presents this difficulty: a spontaneous movement of the soul is inherently and, as it were, logically impossible, since the subject always confronts the obligation to signal that his movement, whatever it may be, is not simply natural or spontaneous, but that it arises only as authorized or condemned by the idea of human rights. What movement of a man toward a woman, or a woman toward a man, can escape this mutilation, this denaturalizing power, included in the "preliminary authorization" of each of its steps? What sincere movement of the soul, in whatever aspect of life, can still be possible as the extension of rights continually extends the domain in which an explicit authorization in conformity with a "guaranty of equality" is required at each moment? Such a society necessarily carries on a ceaseless battle against the "common sense" in which a thousand centuries of human experience have deposited the reference points of human life, "naturalizing" them in the process in one way or another. So now these reference points of common sense indicate not what we should follow but instead what we should flee, not what it is well to aim at but rather what must be avoided.

This would not be so serious if new reference points were instituted, but every new "form of humanity" that might attract human aspirations, supposing that such aspirations could be produced, would immediately be subject to deconstruction or denaturalization in the name of human rights. At the same time as we make sincerity practically impossible by subjecting the slightest movement to the obligation to be explicitly authorized in the name of equality, we throw members of society into a boundless perplexity. We are still obliged, in order to live, to follow at least some indications of common sense—but which ones, when we are summoned from all parts and first of all by the law to distrust any such indication as an arbitrary imposition and a humiliating stereotype? It is thus only weakly, timidly, and not without remorse that we resign ourselves to follow such indications of humanity as have guided us until now, and thanks to which there is still something like a human existence.

One might argue that the movement that carries us forward, and that a powerful segment of public opinion promotes constantly and even fiercely, is less clear or less unified than I maintain. It is true that, while certain constitutive elements of the human world are now radically denaturalized and deprived of any foundation, meaning, or natural purpose (as is particularly the case with the replacement of sex by "gender"), other elements receive the opposite treatment. One thinks first of all of homosexuality. Under the old regime of natural law, homosexuality was considered a "disorder" or a "deviation," that is, a behavior or disposition that ultimately involved the person's choice or the way a person, at the deepest level of the will, orients his or her powers of desire, a choice that was judged to be contrary to the rule inscribed in the physical and moral nature of humanity. Now we demand that this behavior or disposition be regarded as just as "natural" as the heterosexual orientation, as a fact of nature over which the subject has no power and which thus must be regarded and respected as a constitutive part of the very being of the subject. The dominant view of homosexuality seems indeed to go in an opposite direction from the denaturalization that I have invoked. Whereas sex is denaturalized to "gender," homosexuality is naturalized as "sexual orientation": a person is not born woman, but one may be born homosexual, or in any case one discovers oneself as homosexual. Thus, among us, the denaturalization of sexual identity and naturalization of sexual orientation have arisen together.

We can easily see why these two movements are not only simultaneous but in fact are one, each a function of the other. The more sexual difference is naturalized, the more the homosexual orientation seems to go against what nature commands or suggests. Inversely, the more the homosexual orientation is naturalized, the more it diminishes the power or the authority of sexual difference. If homosexual behaviors are judged to be as "natural" as heterosexual behaviors—that is, if sexual orientation is judged to be a matter of indifference—something that makes no difference in the life of the person and in the intimate order of his or her powers, then certainly the difference between the sexes undergoes a major loss of authority, a *diminutio capitis*.

The same correlation appears if we start from the opposite hypothesis. In effect, if the difference between the sexes considered as humanly meaningful is shown to be some kind of "social construction," then sexual desire no longer finds its movement or its destination inscribed in the sexed nature of human beings; it is no longer essentially determined by the sexual difference between the desiring subject and the desired object, but is determined in a random or unpredictable way according to the particular nature of each subject. It is still nature that commands or prevails, but now the nature proper to each individual and no longer human nature understood as representing an order that is valid for all members of the species, with the purely contingent exception of a small number whose individual nature departs from the direction indicated by the common nature. Common nature is henceforth neither trustworthy nor powerful; on the other hand, there is no consideration that can weigh against the nature proper to each individual, which is its own foundation and justification. More precisely, sexual orientation is made a fact of individual nature, and this status not only preserves it from all censure but also removes it from the conversation concerning human things and their complexity: all one can say is that there is nothing to say, since it is a matter of indifference. While the naturalization of sexual difference opened up a great flood of human speech, eliciting the need and nourishing the desire for words and thoughts capable of connecting and, as it were, weaving together the two versions of humanity, the naturalization of sexual orientation removes it from the vital question of humanity.

"Marriage for All"

These remarks may contribute to explaining the prodigious success that the demand for "marriage for all" has had among us of late. How can a demand that has arisen so recently and that concerns only a minority of a minority of the population not only prevail so rapidly with our country's lawmakers but also exercise a power of intimidation and of dismissal of those who are opposed or undecided such as we have not seen in all the history of the movement for human rights? Though the law opening marriage to same-sex couples immediately concerns only a limited number of our fellow citizens, the spiritual stakes of this question are of the greatest importance for all of us. Whereas the demand for tolerance or respect for homosexual couples derives its legitimacy from ordinary sources in our moral nature, the demand for the right to marriage on behalf of these same couples must be considered a metaphysical demand, that is, a demand that bears on the meaning and the whole of human life. Let me explain this somewhat solemn proposition.

Once homosexual orientation is recognized as a fact of nature that is so compact and so "indifferent" that it has nothing to do with reasoned discourse, it becomes the manifest proof that human nature provides no indication concerning the best way to conduct a human life. Considered in this light, homosexuality is nature crying out that there is no natural law. And this is a cry that must be heard but that has too often been smothered by the weight of prejudices or left inaudible in the noisy confusion of human evaluations. Here nature demands the help of positive law. This law must show in the clearest possible manner that all sexual behaviors are equally legitimate and deserve equal respect, or that the equality of sexual behaviors follows analytically from the equality of human rights. What better way is there to demonstrate and to recognize this principle than to open to homosexual couples the very institution that has forever organized sexual difference? Tolerance and social respect are not sufficient, since they leave homosexual couples incapable of marriage, and thus deprived of the public recognition associated with this institution.

When marriage was reserved to heterosexual couples, positive law found support in the natural difference between man and woman and at the same time confirmed and consecrated this difference. The common sense of the species had little need for doctrinal elaboration, but, since the institution of marriage was reserved to heterosexual couples, it implicitly sustained and solemnly manifested that human life is ordered by a natural law. The law opening marriage to same-sex couples is a positive law whose intention targets the very meaning of the human order: the point is to require members of society to recognize by word and deed that there is no natural law, or that the human world can and must be organized without reference to a natural law. Insofar as marriage was the crucial institution of a human world organized according to natural law, the law of which we are speaking aims to overturn or abolish this very order. Henceforth societies living under this law are involved in an experiment that is equally crucial and whose consequences yet to come, public as well as private, will no doubt be commensurate with the audacity or imprudence of what has been done.

This legislation, which directly concerns only a very small portion of society and which has taken hold in our country so fast and, as it were, irresistibly, owes this ascendancy to the ambition I have called metaphysical, the claim to inscribe into positive law the thesis according to which the just or legitimate human order excludes all reference to a natural norm or purpose. But why is it that, although they are for the most part not moved by any personal demand, a great number of our fellow citizens embrace this thesis as a truth so evident and so salutary that it must be imposed by the secular force of the positive law? What is the source of this passionate shared opinion in favor of a proposition that is finally purely philosophical? What is the source of this passionate refusal, which no victory either satisfies or diminishes, to recognize that the meaningful elements of human life are in some way connected with what we call human nature? We will pursue such questions in the next chapter, on the roots and the beginnings of this powerful movement, a movement that aims to organize the human world independently of any reference to a natural order or to the nature of man.

TWO

Counsels of Fear

In the previous chapter I emphasized the central role in the dominant political philosophy of a certain perspective on human things, a perspective that condenses these things into an element of great simplicity and even poverty, the separate living-individual, an element that has nothing specifically human but that, once established in its role as a basis of all that is human, overturns at once our understanding of the human world and the way we intend to organize it. This perspective does not result from focusing on an aspect of the human phenomenon but from reducing the phenomenon to the fact of the separation of separate individuals. This dynamic image-idea provides the point of departure and the point of perspective for a radically new understanding and organization of the human world.[1] We should pause to consider this thought process with some attention.

As I said earlier, the determining and transforming power of this element—the living-individual—results from the fact that *everything that is natural* is gathered and concentrated in it. All the energy and the authority of nature are supposed to reside in this element, which is at once *simple* and *indeterminate*. In these traits it is more like a constituent of the physical than of the human world. It is not the individuality of the individual—the specific content of his particularity—that is considered, but rather the fact of being a separate individual, an individual "in general," thus the very fact of separation. From the point of view of conceptual elaboration, it proceeds from modern natural science, or from the modern philosophy of nature, or, again, taking account of the degree of abstraction of the notion of the "individual," we can say that it proceeds from modern metaphysics. If we consider the notion that originally gave form and life to this element—that is, the notion of *conatus*/endeavor/"effort"—we see that it belongs to reflection or speculation on natural movement or dynamism in general.

In any case, whether one prefers to speak of physics or of metaphysics to designate the field to which the notion of individual-*conatus* belongs, what is constant is that it belongs to a *theoretical* discipline, that it derives from *theoretical* science. It is in effect *entirely* determined *before* the question arises concerning the desirable order of the city or the question of the just action to perform.[2] One might think that the new physics and the promises that were contained in the reduction of the four Aristotelian causes to the efficient cause had such power over minds that the temptation to think the human world, including and first of all political life, in the same terms became irresistible, and that from this point the individual-*conatus*, the living-individual-in-movement, appeared or was elaborated as the causal element that was necessary for the intelligibility and the ordering of the human world. To this plausible conjecture we might add the following complementary conjecture, which is no less plausible but tends in the opposite direction: the adoption of the theoretical point of view on the human world was so irresistible precisely because the meaning of practical philosophy, or simply of practical questioning, had already been lost or irrevocably obscured owing to political and religious circumstances. How in effect can one pose the practical question, the question "What is to be done?," when the authoritative response is twofold, since it may be given by the political authority or by the religious authority? How was the practical question to be posed judiciously when it received *two* responses, sometimes or often incompatible? In any case, the meaning of the process, or rather of the transformation, is clear even though its causes remain mysterious. The meaning of the process, or of the transformation, is the victory of the theoretical point of view in the consideration of the human world.

The Theoretical Point of View and the Downgrading of Politics

It is hard to say which we should admire most, the enormity of the consequences of this transformation or the simplicity of the thought process that sets it off and continually sustains it. This thought process, as I have said, consists in the gathering and the condensation of human traits or characteristics in the separate living-individual, a being that in itself has nothing properly human: each individual contains and bears the whole of humanity, and this assumption or taking-on of humanity is repeated indefinitely or indifferently for each individual. This operation[3] of condensation is illustrated in every way most significantly in the approach of Thomas Hobbes, who means to construct a political order on the exclusive basis of this power-hungry individual-*conatus* as the constitutive and causal element.

Hobbes's approach both postulates the homogeneity of human motives—all human beings obey the same motives—and reduces all these to the desire for power. This approach seems legitimate in itself, since one can say, and Hobbes says in effect, that it is on the basis of the dispositions that are the most widespread among human beings that one has the best chance of constructing a stable political order. But what is most decisive and most contestable in this approach is not what it affirms—that the desire for power is the most fundamental human trait—but what it fails to consider, that is, the very question of action, of how the living-individual is also an acting-agent who confronts the problem of practice. To posit that we are all more or less driven by a desire for power that ceases only with death[4] is to say something powerful and that has a certain verisimilitude, but which leaves aside the perspective and the problems of the agent when he is asking: What is to be done? Hobbes's affirmations concerning human nature do not confront the questions the agent asks himself because Hobbes ignores the reasons and the language that for every person accompany the supposed desire for power, that specify it not only quantitatively or according to intensity but also qualitatively or according to what I will call the ties of reason: under the conditions of political and social life, the desire for power is excited or on the contrary moderated, or in any case *informed*, by the idea of the just that necessarily accompanies it, which gives birth to a whole range of human claims in the public space, claims for which Hobbes shows such a remarkable and damaging disdain. By condensing the springs of action down to the desire for power, Hobbes left no place for action's reasons and postulated or implied that these make no difference or have no determining power. The question posed by Hobbes is no longer the question the agent poses to himself, the practical and "internal" question of reflective choice, but the question posed by the "artisan" or the "*artificer*,"[5] the mechanical or "external" question of the best way to organize the cohabitation or the compatibility of desires for power, desires which are all alike in that they are "without reason."

In this way the theoretical or scientific perspective determines and fixes one element—the living-individual-in-movement—whose content in terms of nature is, one might say, so elevated and so univocal, so determinant and "causal," that there is no more place for properly *practical* reason: this individual's nature is devoid of the interior amplitude and of the indetermination that springs from the meaningful plurality of human motives. Its action is determined in a way that dispenses with deliberation or reflective choice or that reduces these to the smallest share: what sets it in motion is a certain "preference" at which the desiring faculty stops for no particular reason. The individual-*conatus* is not properly an agent; it produces *effects* that resemble actions. Under the regime of the theoretical perspective, or of the new science, reason largely deserts the agent of action in order to assume the standpoint of an observer of human nature, who is also the constructor of the new political order.

The approach that we are trying to bring into focus postulates or presupposes that the human phenomenon considered in its essentials can be viewed *directly* from the theoretical perspective. This postulate or supposition has two inseparable aspects. On the one hand, it is accepted that the phenomenon can be *held* in view, that it does not overflow our vision, or trouble it, or mislead it, which assumes that this knowledge of the human world possesses *from its very first movement* something sufficient and definitive, something, as it were, absolute. This first movement can be so self-assured, so sure of the validity of its "take," only because it proceeds by the simplification and the impoverishment of the phenomenon, which it reduces to the separate individual. The phenomenon offers no rebellion, no resistance, no defiance or reticence to be feared; it is entirely mastered by what will soon be called, with modesty, the "hypothesis." On the other hand, it is implied that the uncertainties of action have no meaningful or decisive character as concerns the understanding of the human world. Practical questions—which are modulations of the originary question, What is to be done?—do not penetrate the philosopher's field of questioning, or only do so as objects subjected to a sovereign point of view, and not as questions that affect the very configuration of the field. Not being "touched" by practical questions, the "new philosopher's" or "new scientist's" reason finds itself incapable of and little interested in entering into the agent's reasons. The intelligence responsible for illuminating the human world disdains getting into the question of action and making itself a practical science or at least making a place for practical science. Declining to illuminate or to guide the agent in his action, it devotes all its strength to determining and then to organizing the *external conditions* of action. In this way Hobbes situates human beings in the framework of equal rights, or equal freedom, by means of the fear inspired by the sovereign. For the rest, as long as they obey the sovereign, the citizens do as they like, the philosopher or scientist having nothing to say or to think about this.

This lowering or relegation of the practical question brings with it a lowering of the status of the political question in which the practical question naturally culminates, since political action is, in the end, "the greatest action," the action with the highest stakes and the greatest risks. If we lower at the outset the status of the question What is to be done?, we necessarily and particularly depreciate that of the question Who governs? If the question What is to be done? is left to the unexamined freedom of the agent, while the philosopher or the scientist is content to busy himself exclusively with determining the conditions of action, then the question Who governs? can be raised, if at all, only after the *conditions* of government have been determined. The question of government—the practical and political question par excellence—has no place, or arises only after the institution that is responsible for and productive of the conditions of action—that is, the sovereign state—has already been established. We see then that the *political* meaning of the modern state is very difficult to grasp, since there are solid reasons for contesting the idea that it is a properly and authentically political institution. It can be considered instead the expression or the concretization of a theoretical point of view on the human world. The sovereignty that defines it operates on a metapolitical or pseudopolitical plane, since it expresses a theoretical viewpoint—a "sovereign" viewpoint—on the human phenomenon. One might say: the state as such does more or does something other than what a human being can do by his action.

It is important not to misunderstand this relegation of the political that is inseparable from the modern theoretical perspective and from the state that expresses and, as it were, institutionalizes this perspective. It would be hard to maintain that Spinoza or Hobbes was less interested in politics than Plato or Aristotle. It would be more correct to say that the moderns expected more from political *organization*, whereas they accorded less importance and meaning to political *action*. They expected more from an organization that they wanted to make less political, that is, less dependent on the actions of members of society and, first of all, the actions of those who govern.

Machiavelli, Idealism, and Realism

The hypertrophy of theory, which is characteristic of the approach we are trying to bring into focus, is ordinarily interpreted as the coming or the introduction of a "realistic" or "scientific" point of view on human things, a point of view that has prevailed decisively—a victory that defines modernity itself—over the "idealistic" point of view, the ancient or Christian perspective of beautiful or good action. The contrast between idealism and realism is extremely suggestive, and it has the additional advantage of providing an interpretation of the quarrel between ancients and moderns that is very favorable to the moderns while still appearing generous towards the ancients. At the same time, to say things with simplicity, it is hard to understand why human beings would have waited so long to "see things as they are."

Let us consider this point. If we look at human things from a "realist" or "scientific" perspective, we do not so much see them "as they are" but rather as they look when we dismiss or hide the acting human being's point of view. In effect we cannot look at human things "as they are," since properly speaking they *are* not; rather, they must be done or "acted." More precisely, "the things that change because they depend on us" cannot be seen as we see "the things that do not change because they do not depend on us," except by removing from the former their practical quality and therefore the specific indetermination that is the source of their mutability. This becomes clearer if we consider the move made by Machiavelli, who is now celebrated as the founder of the realist or even scientific point of view on human action, and specifically on political action. I would like to show that Machiavelli in no way looks at human action "as it is," since he replaces action "as it is"—practical action, one might say—with theoretical action, that is, action as it can be *seen*, action as it can be *taken into view* wholly by the theoretician and that therefore is not obscured or confused by the agent's point of view.

I will comment on what is doubtless the most cited passage in all of Machiavelli's works:

> But since my intent is to write something useful to whoever understands it, it has appeared to me more fitting to go directly to the effectual truth of the thing than to the imagination of it. And many have imagined republics and principalities that have never

been seen or known to exist in truth; for it is so far from how one lives to how one should live that he who lets go of what is done for what should be done learns his ruin rather than his preservation. For a man who wants to make a profession of good in all regards must come to ruin among so many who are not good. Hence it is necessary to a prince, if he wants to maintain himself, to learn to be able not to be good, and to use this and not use it according to necessity.[6]

Machiavelli's point of departure is thus the very big gap ("tanto discosto") between the way people live and the way they should live, or the way people say they should live. Practically everyone can agree with this observation. But what follows from this?, and, especially, what *is to be done* given this observation? The natural approach of the acting human being would be to want to reduce this gap and so, in order effectively to reduce it, to encourage, or persuade, or even force people whose way of life one is concerned with to conduct themselves as they ought, or at least to progress in the right direction as much as possible. In any case this gap only seems so big, and this big gap only urgently requires a solution, in the eyes of someone who is intensely preoccupied with the way we should live and who cannot resign himself to the way people actually behave. It is for the "idealist" that the gap seems so big, whereas, if we give words their natural meaning, the "realist" is content to "take people as they are" without much worrying about what they should be. The spontaneous and sincere debate between the "realist" and the "idealist" on the best response to the chronic failure of human beings in action was portrayed admirably by Molière in the dialogue in *The Misanthrope* between Alceste and Philinte.[7] Machiavelli's approach encounters or creates very different stakes.

In fact, although his first gesture, his first accent, seems to appeal to the idealist in us, immediately afterward Machiavelli turns his back on any action that would seem to be naturally called for by his observation. He does not denounce the hypocritical scribes and Pharisees; he does not overthrow the tables of the money changers; he does not seek "a far-off place on earth where one is free to be an honorable man."[8] What does he do, or, rather, what does he say? He advances this proposition in the form of a maxim that we have read: "He who lets go of what is done for what should be done learns his ruin rather than his preservation." The reader must rub his eyes: Why worry in this way about those who insist absolutely on doing what they should do, since we know—Machiavelli has just reminded us—that most people do something else entirely and since, one might think, they do it precisely in order not to be ruined but to preserve themselves? Who needs Machiavelli's advice and the "effectual truth" of human things that he promises us? What good is it to recommend to people that they act in the way they act spontaneously? The fate of a few "idealists" or of some Don Quixote may be the stuff of tragedy, or rather no doubt of comedy, but it is quite hard to see what untold motive their misfortune might provide, what "news" either good or bad it might bring, to someone who conforms to the ordinary course of human things and conducts himself in the usual way of those born of woman.

One might say that Machiavelli is simply asking us to regard what people do without indignation or a desire for reform, since what they should do is only a dream and a chimera. Surely it is not good to take more than one's share, but since people regularly do so, it is reasonable to steal at least when the gain justifies the risk. This in sum would be the realist's commandment. There is *something* of this in Machiavelli, but, again, why urge people to do what most of them would do anyway? Why carry coal to Newcastle? Still less can we attribute such platitudes to Machiavelli given that this great mind boasts of bringing human beings a *new* truth.

We must return to the great "gap" between what people do and what they should do. As I emphasized at the outset, Machiavelli does not draw the *practical* consequences from this observation that it naturally calls for, that is, the consequences that would be drawn by an agent truly concerned with practice and effectively preoccupied with doing good and performing good actions. At the same time there is no doubt that the recognition of this "gap" is indeed the starting point, or at least a decisive point of support in his approach. It is therefore reasonable to suppose that in Machiavelli's eyes this gap is evidence less of a practical failure of human beings—of a "sin" by them—than what one might call a gnoseological failure. It is not so much that people do not succeed in doing what they should do; the decisive point is rather that they do not achieve clarity on what they do. They do not know what they do, and for this Machiavelli does not forgive them.

Just what, more precisely, is this ignorance or misunderstanding of the self? I would summarize things as follows: on the one hand, human beings cannot help doing what they do; on the other, they cannot help wanting in some way to do what they should do. At the same times as they do what they do, which is nothing to be proud of, they speak as if they were doing what they should do; often they even find a way to imagine that they are in fact doing what they should. The consequence of this division of the mind or duplicity is that they see double and that, without of course doing what they should do, they do badly what it is that they do. Thus, what they should do, which is summed up in the precepts of natural law or of morality, is not so much what they fail to do, what they do not succeed in attaining or respecting, but rather something that troubles their perspective and falsifies their vision, and so hinders or diverts or in any case diminishes their powers. Human beings cheerfully disobey natural law as soon as it hampers their desires, but they are sufficiently intimidated by it that they do not go all the way in what they have started. Morality weakens them without correcting them. The law that is supposed to regulate their action only deprives it of the energy or scope of which it was capable. This explains why an incestuous and parricide *condottiere*[9] dared not raise his hand against Pope Julius II, who had imprudently put his fate in the former's hands. The *condottiere* did not accomplish the great action that the circumstances called for, the great action that the circumstances had delivered, one might say, on a silver platter.[10]

To be sure, Machiavelli never treats natural law thematically. Still, when he warns the candidate-prince that "men forget the death of a father more quickly than the loss of a patrimony,"[11] he is invoking at once the commandments of natural law and the irregular relationship between human beings and this law. He only considers it in certain concrete circumstances, where it is present and more or less active in the conscience of agents. He does not criticize it as such, but in every way possible he incites his reader not to be intimidated by it in any case where it might come between the agent and an action worthy of being undertaken. Machiavelli does not suggest that the natural law is invalid itself and that it would be good or at least indifferent to kill and to pillage. There are prohibitions and recommendations that belong to the human condition and that taken together constitute the natural law, and it is good or useful that people in general have a certain respect for the commandments of this law, which protects their "humanity."[12] But it belongs to those who have the ambition to act on a large scale not to allow themselves to be stopped by this law when it would turn them away from a great and necessary action: they must be ready and "know how to enter into evil" if they are constrained to do so—*sapere intrare nel male, necessitato.*[13] Machiavelli cannot wish for the generalization of this audacity, since the success of the prince endowed with *virtù*—the "good effects" of his bad actions—depends upon the honest pusillanimity that constitutes the "goodness" of the many. The great and brutal action of the prince, which often consists in "executions," can produce its purging and pacifying effects only because its greatness and brutality break with the horizon of expectation of the many, which is circumscribed by natural law. The people did not expect *that*, and because surprise is accompanied by a certain admiration, they can hide the fear they feel from themselves, the fear that is the main cause of the efficaciousness of the prince's action.[14]

Thus natural or moral law, which hinders and weakens people of action, is, according to Machiavelli, insufficient for gathering human beings together. The vague wish to do what is right that morality arouses has little power over human desires that are in themselves unlimited. One might perhaps say that it brings people together imaginatively or that it arises from human imagination, not from the special imagination of poets but from the general imagination of the species as shaped by the wise people—philosophers or prophets— who conceive their "imaginary republics." In its simplest and perhaps most profound essence, the natural law is the way human beings *imagine* that they are brought together, or the way they conceive the *imaginary* cause of their union.

According to Machiavelli, it is important and indeed urgent to awaken them from this false dream of unity. There are not so many ways to do this; in the end there is only one, and that is to make them afraid, as we have already seen. The only thing that *effectively* gathers people together is fear. Fear is, to be sure, a strange way to gather human beings, by making each person feel his limitless preference for himself. Whereas natural law brought people together imaginatively while leaving them passive and separate, fear really unites them by forcing each individual to "recognize himself," that is, to leave behind the imaginary associations in which his capacities for action are invested and lost.

Here arises an objection, or a complication. Natural law and fear, it may be argued, are not mutually exclusive, since most human beings are at least *intimidated* by the commandments of natural law—which is moreover the main source of their mediocre obedience to authority as well as of the setbacks they suffer in their political enterprises, as we have seen in the case of the petty tyrant of Perugia. It is indeed precisely this fear of natural law or of the gods who guarantee it that Machiavelli intends to drive from the hearts or minds of those he addresses; in this way they will be able usefully to frighten those who remain intimidated by natural law, and who doubtless will always be the greater number.

I will sum up the gnoseological situation that Machiavelli proposes to sort out and to reform in the following way: If human beings are victims of a great gap between what they do and what they should do; if they continually produce this great gap that confuses their outlook and hinders their action; if, to be brief, they do not know what they are doing, this is because they are prisoners of this knot in which fear of death is interwoven with fear of natural or divine law—the two adjectives are interchangeable here because what these two laws or two types of law have in common (besides the fact that they include largely the same commandments) is that their commandments are *produced by no one*, in any case by no living human being, even though it is of course human beings who administer their interpretation and execution. In our context, it seems to me that what most decisively determines Machiavelli's analysis as well as his prescriptions is the contrast between, on the one hand, the fear produced by a person or group of persons engaged in a great action, the fear produced by one or more agents who are *determinate* and *visible*, and, on the other hand, the fear of a commandment given by no one and that everyone senses vaguely it would be good or necessary or imperative to obey—that is, a commandment from a source that is *invisible* and humanly *indeterminate* or *indeterminable*. What orders Machiavelli's perspective is the polarity between a humanity that is poorly unified and torpid, a prisoner of a natural law that is protective but paralyzing, and certain human agents of a new kind whom this law no longer intimidates, and who moreover are up to the task of conducting their action in a manner fully adequate to what the situation at once authorizes and commands.

We see how Machiavelli deals with the great "gap" that provides the point of departure for his approach, the point from which we have ourselves begun. As I have emphasized, Machiavelli does not respond to this "gap" or seek to reduce it *practically* by indicating paths to a better way of acting—to a more just or wise way—nor, moreover, by suggesting, as will other moralists and political writers, that the goal be lowered and that we not aim at what is too high and impossible to attain.[15] He focuses on this gap and fixes or determines it, and, rather than seeking to suppress or at least to reduce it, he seeks a way around the domain in which this gap is necessarily produced, that is, the domain of practice itself. This gap sums up the practical problem and the traditional formulation of the practical problem, a formulation that Machiavelli proposes to leave behind and from which he proposes to emancipate us. This gap is produced necessarily by the shaky way in which human beings negotiate their conduct, caught as they are between their limitless and essentially irresistible desires and the commandments of natural law that intimidate them without governing them. As paradoxical as it may seem, in order to escape the practical stagnation in which he sees humanity languishing, Machiavelli elaborates and promotes a nonpractical view of action—an action greater than action, or in any case an action no longer subject to the limits that spring from the fact that action is naturally produced by an agent and that it depends therefore on the virtuous or vicious dispositions of this agent, an action no longer determined and limited by the dispositions and ends of the *agent* but instead opened up to all the possibilities inherent in the *situation*.

We see how emancipation with respect to the practical perspective and the point of view of the agent seems considerably to enlarge the field of possible actions; for, whereas the exploitation of the possibilities of the situation has been constrained by the dispositions and reasons of the agent, Machiavelli imagines that all the possibilities of the situation might be opened to an agent who may be said to be without quality, one capable of changing "as the winds of fortune and variations of things command him"[16]—in brief, an agent unencumbered by the limits that define him as an agent. The possibilities of the situation, or the circumstances, rather than being a component of practical reasoning, a component that is indispensable but secondary because there are circumstances only for someone who acts in a certain way and with a certain goal, now rise to the first rank and exist, so to speak, in themselves, or as sufficient to themselves. This is possible only if one can posit circumstances independently of any action envisaged by a definite agent, thus only if the circumstances can be the object of a purely *theoretical* regard. It is by this inversion of the relation between the agent and the circumstances of his action that Machiavelli violently subjects the human world to theoretical reason.

The consequence of Machiavelli's approach is that, although the field of action seems to expand considerably, it becomes indeterminate at the same time and for the same reasons. Paradoxically, it is impossible to derive a "Machiavellian politics" from Machiavelli's work. What were his political projects? Did the great "realist" really believe that Italy was ripe for unity?[17] Was the pope the enemy to be liquidated, as he regretted that Giovampagolo had not dared to do? Or was he the only person capable of unifying Italy against the barbarians, as he *seems* to suggest several times? Such questions are fascinating but ultimately vain. By disdaining the question of the limited indetermination proper to action performed by an agent whose dispositions as well as his ends are relatively stable, by treating with contempt the indetermination that is specifically characteristic of practice, Machiavelli produces an indetermination of an unprecedented extent and quality, an indetermination that can be called limitless. But looking at the world as the immense and indeterminate sum of the circumstances of all possible actions—a phrase in which the adjective has become radically stronger than the noun—he invites the undertaking of an action that answers to the limitless quality of these possibilities, an action that therefore requires not an agent determined by his dispositions and his reasons but, on the contrary, an agent who makes himself capable of *all* possible action by overturning the limits inherent in his character as an agent.

Although it has always been and will always be impossible to derive a political project from Machiavelli's own words, there is no question of underestimating the effects of his words on political thought and life. By emancipating the human enterprise from all positive reference to natural law, and by opening up an impassable chasm between the domain of the new *possible* action and the observable condition of human beings, in which the natural law deprives their action of energy and of edge, Machiavelli invites us to reconstitute the political order from top to bottom and to deliver to human beings the great secret of the operation: fear, appropriately applied, will be an advantageous substitute for law. Cutting through the knot where the fear of death is interwoven with the fear of the law, he isolates in all its purity, I am inclined to say, the power of fear—its shaping and founding power. There is no question of making Machiavelli out as a thinker of "individualism." Still, with an acuity that continues to trouble us, he shows us fear as applied or manipulated by the prince, or by the republican magistrate, seeking out each individual at the point where he or she forgets the law or, more generally, is left with no orienting factor but this very fear. Fear has ceased to be one affect among others that are equally powerful, an affect that has its place in the disposition of affects; instead the fear that one human being arouses in another appears as the greatest power among human beings. This power consists not only in making some people conform to the will of others but, more profoundly, in producing in an absolute sense one who is as independent from all law as the most exalted prince. According to what might be called its most radical or most original definition, the individual is the being whose most active and deepest orienting factor is fear, especially fear of violent death at the hands of others.

By making natural law into this factor, which is at once very strong and very weak, and under whose power human action is obscured and encumbered, Machiavelli contributed more than any other author to the discrediting of natural law. He brought out the opacity and viscosity of this hobbled existence by deploying the polarity—a brilliant polarity that will continue to control if not effectively to enlighten us—between, on the one hand, an action that is greater than action and that despises law, and, on the other, a passion more penetrating than any other and that makes us forget the law. By making the gap between what people do and what they should do the stumbling block that demands that we leave the very plane of practical life, with its inevitable uncertainty and incompetence, Machiavelli instilled in us an excessive desire for clarity that, rather than opening us up to unprecedented domains, closes us off from access to the field of practical life, that is, of action under law, a field in which we indeed observe a great gap between what people do and what they should do.

The Human Condition and the Christian Condition

It remains for me to touch the most delicate point of the situation, that is, of Machiavelli's analysis and of his dispositions or intentions.

Is this practical condition of which I have spoken—the condition that Machiavelli invites us to overcome, that is, the condition in which members of society, intimidated by natural law, waste or divide their powers by investing them in imaginary republics—is this a general condition of humanity as such, or is it not rather the special condition of humanity as marked by what Machiavelli called "our religion," that is, the Christian religion? Many passages from *The Prince* and especially from *The Discourses* incline us decidedly toward the latter alternative. I do not believe, however, that the question is so clear, since, although Machiavelli indeed insists on the deleterious effects of Christianity in comparison with the bracing effects of pagan religion, he is still left to account for the fact that human beings have proven so well disposed toward the new religion, which made its earliest and decisive conquests *without arms*. If it appears that human capacities have been degraded by Christianity, then this is because the natural condition of human beings was open to Christian influence, that is, that Christianity found nature to be a favorable terrain. There thus cannot be a significant difference between "the human condition" and the "Christian condition." One might say more precisely that Christianity expresses and intensifies the practical condition of humanity, the difficulty of a humanity exposed to the "big gap" of which we have already had much to say, a humanity whose strength is divided between its obstructed nature and an imaginary political and religious life. Christianity expresses and aggravates the weakness and the incompetence of human action, placing Christians in what Machiavelli suggestively calls an *ambizioso ozio*, an ambitious carelessness or irresponsibility, one might perhaps say a pretentious passivity, a disposition that takes to its limits the gap between words and actions to which human beings are naturally led or condemned.[18] The most corrupting consequence of this redoubled passivity is that, among Christians, in Machiavelli's piercing words, "it is evil to speak evil of evil."[19] This laziness or pusillanimity discourages speech as well as action, and most especially action tied to speech, thus political action, in the Christian world.

If the Christian religion only expresses and thereby aggravates the natural condition of humanity, then it makes sense that in order to overcome *Christian* inaction or passivity it would be necessary somehow to overcome the *human* condition, that is, more precisely, as we have been arguing, to overcome the *practical* condition that defines human life, to recover action, but to do this by producing an unprecedented action, one that is no longer guided and thus limited by practical reasoning, by "reflective choice." Now the condition of practice, in a Christian context, is distilled in the notion of *conscience*, the tribunal before which each person is capable of judging himself as God judges him, provided that his conscience is active and well informed. Thus, for Machiavelli, to overcome and leave behind the human condition is to *dismiss conscience*, which he does very explicitly and even emphatically, particularly when he urges the prince, as we have seen, to "learn to be able not to be good" and to "know how to enter into evil" when necessary.[20]

What is most significant in Machiavelli's repeated advice is not the fact that he invites the prince to do evil when circumstances require it, but that he asks him for this reason to renounce his conscience *in advance*, to dismiss in advance the natural guide and judge of human actions. It is one thing to say that the necessities of action risk leading you to act in a way that will shock your conscience; it is another to say: learn not to be good even before necessity requires this of you. Such an apprenticeship can only mean in effect the obliteration of conscience itself. It is this erasure or eradication of conscience, of this human capacity brought to light only in a Christian context, that sums up and fulfills the leaving behind of the practical condition that Machiavelli encourages and promotes.[21] The erasure or eradication of the *internal* guide and judge leads to the search for *external* orienting factors, that is, elements *in the world* such as it is grasped no longer according to practical dispositions but according to various *theoretical* perspectives. The two great versions of the world considered theoretically can be summed up by the notions *nature* and *history*. Accordingly, it is by their "science of nature" or their "science of history" that the moderns will strive more and more to guide and to justify their actions, their unprecedented actions, actions that are greater and other than actions, that is, their *revolutions*.

At the same time—as it were, at the very same moment when Machiavelli was making his move on the basis of a reinterpretation of ancient and modern political experience—Luther was making an analogous or parallel move on the basis of a reinterpretation of the Christian religious experience. There can be no question here of entering casually into the great, the immense question of the

Reformation. Still, it would be a pity to forgo the insight—at once a complement and a confirmation—provided by Luther's very remarkable approach. Here I will only note what is directly relevant to my subject. In itself, the principle of "grace alone"—*sola gratia*—does no more than to recall and emphasize God's sovereign initiative as it is affirmed and celebrated by Christian revelation. The distinctive point of the Lutheran Reformation is focused on the principle of "faith alone"—*sola fide*—by which Luther escapes from the impasse of a life haunted by awareness of sin. By the leap of faith, he achieves a confidence or a certitude—a *fiducia*—that, while it does not of course belong to the theoretical order, tends to remove the believer from the practical order, insofar as this certitude accedes *immediately* to a God whose grace does not really transform or sanctify the sinner, but shields the sinner from God's wrath by taking the sin upon himself. One might say: where there had been an *acting* Christian, or a Christian *agent*, now there is simply a *believer*.

Here it is indispensable to consider Luther's very words with some attention. I will take them from a long discussion in which the Reformer intends to refute Erasmus's diatribe, entitled *On Free Will*. Luther blames Erasmus for a radically erroneous understanding of the law. Since Scripture abounds in imperative verbs, since it is rich in commandments, Erasmus concludes that a human being is in principle capable of obeying these commandments, which otherwise would be vain.[22] Luther responds to this practical understanding of the commandments and the law by opposing to it an altogether different understanding, one to which the adjective "gnoseological" would be particularly well suited: "The whole meaning and purpose of the law is simply to furnish knowledge, and that of nothing but sin; it is not to reveal or to confer any power."[23] Or again: "What comes through the law is not righteousness but knowledge of sin. It is the task, function, and effect of the law to be a light to the ignorant and blind, but such a light as reveals sickness, sin, evil, death, hell, the wrath of God, though it affords no help and brings no deliverance from these, but is content to have revealed them. Then, when a man becomes aware of the disease of sin, he is troubled, distressed, even in despair."[24] Thus, according to Luther, the law does not guide us, does not show us the way; it does not command actions that, however difficult or even impossible to accomplish without the help of grace, would nevertheless offer a pertinent object for us to aim at and to strive for. The despair brought about by the law throws us outside the regime of action, into a state of dereliction from which we can escape only by means wholly other than an action or a course of action. This means is thus *faith alone*.

What interests us here is the way Luther understands the meaning of the act of faith, of the gesture of "faith alone." Without entering into the labyrinth of theological controversies, I cannot avoid saying a word concerning the contending positions. According to the traditional Catholic analysis, faith is an act of the intellect commanded by the will, which is itself moved by grace, an act of the intellect that gives its consent to the *salutary truth*, that is, to the true good that makes a human being happy.[25] From this perspective, faith aims inseparably at an objective truth and an objective good, to be sure a good that concerns me, that is indeed my good, but this as a consequence of my belonging to the human family that is the object of divine benevolence. I believe that God alone has the power to save, that I need his grace as do all human beings, who are all sinners, and this is the truth to which I adhere in the act of faith. The question whether I myself am or will be "saved" is a question that cannot fail to interest me deeply, but it does not enter as such into the act of faith. Where *my* salvation is concerned, I appeal to specific criteria, and first of all precisely God's law such as the authority of the church explains and administers it. The question of *my* salvation is here inseparable from the question of my *actions*, or my *conduct*, as these are directed and judged by my *conscience*, a conscience that is more or less informed, more or less awakened, more or less scrupulous; and this direction and judgment normally require the help of the sacraments and of the church as an institution. Absent a particular revelation, the most I can hope in this order of things is to arrive at a "reasonable hope" of being saved. Though the context may be very special—eternal salvation!—the Christian finds himself in the ordinary and common condition of the agent who can do no better than to act in such a way as to have a reasonable hope of achieving his ends.[26]

For Luther, of course, all that is a tissue of absurdities embroidered by the devil. For him, I cannot really believe, I cannot seriously believe, unless I believe that *I* am saved. Only the certainty of *my* salvation guarantees the authenticity of my faith. Luther opposes this certainty to the uncertainty of those who judge their own actions according to their conscience:

> Ask all the exercisers of free choice to a man, and if you are able to show me one who can sincerely and honestly say with regard to any effort or endeavor of his own, "I know that this pleases God," I will acknowledge myself conquered. . . . Now, if this glory is lacking, so that the conscience dare not say for certain or with confidence that "this pleases God," then it is certain it does not please God. For as a man believes, so it is with him, and in this case he does not believe with certainty that he pleases God, although it is necessary to do so, because the offense of unbelief lies precisely in having doubts about the favor of God, who wishes us to believe with the utmost possible certainty that he is favorable.[27]

As this long passage adequately indicates, what Luther means by the term "free will" is what might be called the natural regime of conscience. It is the acting person's regime of conscience, which has nothing to do with certainty, that Luther passionately rejects, owing to the imperious need he feels for complete certainty. This certainty will be the result of the believer's effort of faith; the believer wants to believe he is saved and effectively finds certainty in his will to be certain. The virtue of faith tends to become an art of believing, and the believer a virtuoso of faith.[28]

Luther wanted to escape what was for him the anguished half-light of practical life and to deliver Christians from it. So he orders the human world by juxtaposing contraries or opposites, but contraries or opposites that are or at least appear to be equally clear. Rather than being engaged along a path of improvement, the fragile steps along which the conscience measures with prudence and justice, the Christian, according to Luther, regards himself as *at the same time* righteous and sinner, *simil justus et peccator*. Similarly, while God is supremely hidden, Scripture is perfectly clear, and this is why Christians do not need the mediation of the pope or of the doctors of the church.[29] Again, in order to exclude all ambiguity, Luther introduces a division and an opposition interior to God himself, between the God who is preached, revealed, offered, and the object of worship and the God who is not preached, not revealed, not offered, not the object of worship, in short the hidden God; between the Word of God and God himself; and, finally, between God incarnate and the hidden God.[30] Since the received practice of Christian life depends on the more or less well-maintained balance between the internal conscience of the Christian and the authority of the visible church, Luther attacks with equal vigor these two principles, whose intrinsic solidarity, he discerns, is the condition of a life under the law. In his view, the authority of the visible church captures the consciences of the people in the snare of false laws and false sins, filling the world with hypocrites, while it would be so simple to regulate external acts by the external constraints of the civil magistrate.[31] Instead of the internal conscience perversely tied to the visible church, there is the separation and complementarity of the invisible church and the civil magistrate. The conscience that linked the agent to the visible church is replaced by the conscience liberated by the gospel, that is, by "Christian freedom," which judges well only by judging without the law or outside the law.[32] The reformed conscience liberates the believer from the law that furnished the main orienting criterion of the practical conscience. The reformed Christian, a virtuoso of faith, finds his completion as a *believer*, rejecting the *acting* Christian, the Christian *agent*, as a Christian blasphemer and a hypocrite, whom he sees as entangled in the bonds of a conscience in bondage. The life of the believer, oriented by faith alone, lifts itself victoriously up above the level of practical life, where the old man, Christian or non-Christian, is subjected to the impossible obligations of the law.

Thus Luther, like Machiavelli, seeks and postulates an exit from and an access beyond the practical condition of humanity, a condition which for both is characterized by a supremely shocking and decisively illuminating gap between the real life of human beings and the law that they intend or pretend to follow. Though Machiavelli and Luther seek solutions in two very different directions, one in the anticipation of necessity and the disposition to "enter into evil" when necessary, the other in the leap of faith that takes hold of God's righteousness and covers itself with it as with a cloak, they both reject practical conscience as it has been brought to light in the Christian world—the internal judge capable of measuring the distance between the way one lives and the way we ought to live, and thus of guiding our improvement. Both Luther and Machiavelli despaired of the human agent's capacity for improvement when this agent is prisoner of the bonds of a bound conscience. Since the *nature* of the human being or of the Christian cannot really be improved or made more perfect, we can only dare radically to change the *condition* of the human being or of the Christian, and this by a supremely audacious gesture that removes them from their practical condition or lifts them above it. Whether a prince gifted with *virtù* or a virtuoso of faith, this new human being will approach the conduct of life in an unprecedented fashion; while leaving human nature to its inertia or its insurmountable imperfection, this new approach will introduce human beings into a new state that will allow them to experience an *unlimited* confidence in the promise they make to themselves. Disdaining the gap between life and the law and leaving behind the burdens and the shame of practical life, this new human being undertakes an exercise of humanity that gives access not to a good that his conscience might situate on the gradient of perfection but to a "better" that knows no criterion of the good or the better, a "better" that has no measure. And yet, by detaching from the practical conscience what must henceforth be the main activity of humanity—the virtuosity either of action or of faith—do we not run the risk of losing sight entirely of the "gap" that the practical conscience once discerned and measured, and thus of no longer knowing from what or for what we have "liberated" ourselves?

THREE

The Order of the State without Right or Law

We must return to an affect, a passion, with which we have already been much concerned, that is, fear. It has disappeared from the intellectual framework that helps us to conceive the collective order and to organize common life. Someone establishing an index of the main notions of political liberalism and of representative government or of modern democracy could omit the entry "fear" without any risk of scandal. In fact its absence would not be noticed; it is rather the presence of this notion that would surprise or even shock. Such an off-putting, indeed chilling affect as fear would cast a sinister shadow over the architecture of the positive and even cheerful notions that organize modern politics. More profoundly, whereas the usual notions are resolutely abstract, whether it is a question of "human rights," of "representation," of "material and moral interests," or further of "separation of powers," fear is something concrete, painfully concrete one might say, something that concretely designates a primordial component of *human nature* that can be observed or experienced by each of us. In fact, however much we may want to be the sovereign authors of the human order and to depend on nothing but our freedom, the construction of modern politics would never have been able to take hold without deriving support from our *nature*, and more precisely from the *passivity* of our nature, as it imposes itself on us especially in the affect of fear. It is this decisive role of our nature in its passivity under the aspect of fear that the reading of Machiavelli and Hobbes puts before our eyes.

At the same time, it is true that it is hard for us to conceive that such a complex and refined edifice as the modern political order could be based on something so simple—so vulgar, one is tempted to say—as fear. Not only is our vanity offended, but our good sense pushes back. One person frightens someone; another is frightened; and maybe the second responds by frightening the first. How can a principle of order be derived from this tangle of passions? It is in fact hazardous, as I have emphasized, to make conjectures concerning Machiavelli's political intentions or projects; it is even impossible to "derive a political teaching" from this supposedly "realist" work. And yet Thomas Hobbes found the way to render Machiavelli's perspective—I was going to say Machiavelli's *reformation*—at once *moral* and *practicable*, without in any way backing off from the primacy of fear, indeed while making the use of fear thematic and systematic. He could not have based a rigorous approach on fear, he could not have based an institution on a radically new type of fear, an institution destined to give modern life its form—that is, the state— if he had not succeeded at the same time in *moralizing* fear, in giving it a moral function and so to speak a moral mission. Hobbes accomplished this task by removing fear from all dependency in relation to natural law, however this law might be conceived. Far from leaving the affect of fear under a rule that would guide the way in which this affect must be mastered and that might require, for example, that the city inculcate virtues such as courage in its citizens, he puts fear in the position of a cause, of a moral or rather *moralizing* cause: it is the affect itself—the passion of fear, that is—that is the spring or the pivot of what Hobbes again calls the natural law, a "natural law" that is not properly a law but rather, as Hobbes readily admits, a "conclusion" or a "theorem" derived from the human fear of death.[1]

How then does he proceed? As I said, he gives fear a moral function and even a moral mission; he brings out the *moralizing* potential of this affect. Not only is fear the most constant, the most powerful, and thus the most trustworthy human motive, but it has the singular virtue of repressing the most toxic affect of the human species as well as of the individuals that compose it, the affect Hobbes designates by the term "pride," which prevents "every man [from acknowledging the] other for his Equall by Nature."[2] By this he means the irresistible tendency of the human heart that causes human beings ceaselessly to recount dangerously seductive stories about themselves, each person with his particular stories as well as the stories of the human race in general. By repressing vainglory and pride, fear not only promises and produces peace among members of society and thus guarantees external order; it also resists the dominance of error and falsity internal to every person, that is, the ambitious and pretentious imagination of those who believe and those who believe in themselves (and these are often the same)—that is, the imagination of those who believe that the gods look upon them with particular benevolence and who therefore are ready to make themselves the spokespersons of divinity and the imagination of those who think themselves superior to others in some way and for whom this superiority entitles them to command others or to put themselves above them.

It is impossible to mistake not only the moral component of Hobbes's approach but also the intensity of his moral tone. But it is harder precisely to discern the status and, as it were, the site of this morality. The moral order is born for Hobbes from the encounter between the person who frightens and the one who is afraid, that is, between two figures devoid of morality, understanding the term "morality" here as the orientation that is at least claimed according to a rule posited or received in advance. One who fears, or whom it is important to frighten, is not only without morality but is driven by the most ruleless human passion, that is, *pride*. We know nothing of the motive or intention of the one who frightens, the sovereign or the state; our knowledge is limited to the happy effect of that person's action, that is, peace. Thus the morality that Hobbes is so careful to bring about and that the modern state really produces is an *effect* of morality—the moral effect of the encounter or the dynamic between two figures who are themselves devoid of morality.

Man Is the Being with Rights

This dynamic devoid of intrinsic morality, from which results and which produces the new institution, is rooted in the natural human condition, which is itself devoid of intrinsic morality. It is well known that the state of nature, or of the war of all against all, which is the war of each individual against every other individual, is a lawless state, a condition devoid of any law whatsoever.[3] But why, then, given that there is no law, would there be right or rights? What in particular is the meaning of the right proper to the state of nature, the right of every individual to everything, including others' bodies[4]—the *jus in omnia*—especially given that *all* are bearers of this right? What in effect can be the meaning of a right that, rather than distinguishing and distributing things and persons, expresses and confirms a confusion devoid of the least seed of order? When it is said that all have a right to everything, does this not mean finally that no one has a right to anything? One might answer that this is indeed the case and that it is precisely for this reason that it is necessary to leave the state of nature. Granted, but if it is only outside the state of nature that individuals have an effective right to certain things, that means it is pointless to speak of "rights" in the state of nature, especially a right to all things. How can one have a right when the affirmation of a right or of rights neither implies nor allows any determination, even the most approximative, either from the side of the person or of the thing? The main difficulty is not that right in the Hobbesian state of nature has no reality or effectiveness; it is that it has no meaning:[5] there is no way to put it in words, except in words that have no meaning, such as the phrase *jus in omnia*.

These objections do not apply only to the teachings of modern natural right, which could not have been elaborated without the "hypothesis" of a "state of nature." Since these teachings provided the axioms of our public philosophy, this philosophy is vulnerable to the same objections, objections that do not spare the sacred sentence contained in the first article of the Declaration of the Rights of Man and of the Citizen: "Human beings are born and remain free and equal in rights." To be sure, there is no mention here of a right of all to everything, but the familiarity and the authority of the proposition cannot hide its vertiginous indeterminacy, or rather its determination-defying character. Indefinite rights are here attached to indefinite individuals—to each and to all. Now, one might say that this indetermination is inseparable from the universality of the principle. This is true, but so is the reverse: the universality proper to the doctrine of human rights is inseparable from this indetermination, this active power of producing indetermination. Whatever the concrete arrangements put in place by human beings, these are exposed in advance to contestation and to claims that have no limit either on the side of the subject of rights or on that of the matter of rights. Since every social arrangement holds together and unites, under some *determinate* form, certain *determinate* persons and *determinate* goods, services, or activities, all social arrangements are vulnerable to a contestation, and finally to a partial or total *negation* that can always claim to be legitimate and just since it is derived from human rights. The same principle that today grounds *this* claim of rights will sooner or later justify a more radical claim of more extensive rights. This extension is never just an extension, that is, an augmentation of the number of rights bearers; it necessarily involves a qualitative change of institution or of association, a change that can be immensely positive[6] but can also prove damaging when the increasingly exclusive preoccupation with rights in the end obscures the purpose of the institution and undermines its effectiveness.

This ambivalence in the extension of human rights is most often ignored. We suppose that the extension of rights in itself means progress, improvement, the attainment of a higher quality of human association. This is to underestimate the complexity of social, political, and moral life. The extension of rights, the openness to "new rights," can never constitute more than half of our task. We are in effect bound beforehand to order the common world by rules or by laws that *determine* such order and that must be derived from sources other than human rights. The declaration and promotion of human rights in effect presupposes the *prior* existence of a human world *already ordered* according to rules and purposes that cannot be derived simply from human rights. If we wish, for example, to extend rights of access to the university in a judicious way, it is important first to have a somewhat clear idea of the meaning of the university as an institution. If "new rights" are going to mean effective social and moral progress, then they must not obscure or damage the meaning of the institution to which we wish to give wider access. Human rights by themselves provide no positive determination of the contents, or of the "goods," of human life; they may concern indiscriminately actions, functions, status, qualifications, goods, services, or any yet unnamed object to which a claim that is unforeseeable today might wish tomorrow to attach a right, a "new right." Once established in its exclusive legitimacy, the idea of rights tends to become an empty form in search of its matter, and everything, literally everything, can become matter for this form. Any and all aspects of human life, from the most evident to the most secret, are henceforth open to a legitimate claim. The infinitely complex and differentiated architecture of life is given over to a *right of access* indifferent to this complexity. To declare human rights in a way that is perfectly indeterminate and actively resistant to determination is to grant to just anyone the formal authorization to *claim* whatever thing in the human world he judges or feels he has a right to. And why would not everyone demand his right to all things, since all things have been declared a matter of human rights? Thus the *jus in omnia* that could find no meaning in the state of nature where everything was still indeterminate, finds a particularly ample and troubling meaning in our regime of rights, since what is delivered over to a *jus omnium in omnia* are all the determinations, all the qualities, all the aspects of an actually existing world. All concretely human forms, whether it is a question of the nation, the family, the university, or of any institution that shelters and produces a determinate human good, are delivered up to a *claim* that is not concerned to have rhyme or reason because it has been given an unlimited authorization in advance.

In order to give some minimal plausibility to this hypothesis or postulate of a condition characterized by rights without law, or of man defined as the being with rights, theoreticians of modern natural right have had to make much of certain traits of the state of nature understood as a war of everyone against everyone. In effect, in such a situation it would be quite difficult in practice to incriminate someone for some action he had committed and thus to contest his "right" to act in this way, since he could always more or less plausibly claim the excuse of legitimate self-defense. One can grant the argument, even though the conditions of the state of war do not eliminate all distinctions among actions, as Hobbes himself recognized with his noted honesty. But even if, in certain violent situations, all actions tend to resemble each other in their violence, it takes a lawyer's trick to assimilate the act of one who kills in self-defense to the act of one who attacks in order to kill. Moreover, "legitimate self-defense" itself does not properly define a "right," or only in a very restricted or technical sense. The situation called legitimate self-defense cancels the punishable character of an act contrary to the law that forbids murder or battery. To say that one has "the right of self-defense" does not mean that one has precisely the "right to kill" in defending oneself. It means rather that one is immune from penalty, or acquitted, if one has killed or wounded one's attacker while defending against him. The infraction is determined without being punishable. The acquittal demanded by the lawyer is conditional on a very meticulous and even mistrustful examination of the circumstances, with particular attention given to the "proportionality" of the self-defense in relation to the attack.

We see, then, that the recognition of a situation of legitimate self-defense by no means reveals a "right" somehow prior to all law, but rather a properly exceptional suspension of the application of the law that forbids murder and determines the punishment of the murderer—a law that does not cease to be valid even though its application is suspended, exceptionally or extraordinarily. How, moreover, could this "right," supposing it is valid, constitute the source or provide the type of rights that are pertinent in social and political life, which requires the application of principles that are much more complex and refined than the right to persevere in being or to preserve oneself—which, if we had to name the rights bearer, is less a right of a human being than the right of a *conatus*? In any case, the abusive interpretation of the "legitimate right of self-defense," extended to the whole of human rights, has greatly contributed to obscuring our vision of social and political life. What is lost from view in particular is the determining and specific role of the law as a rule of action, since right, now understood as prior to and independent from law, presents itself to us as a sufficient principle of action, a function that it can in no way fulfill.

Let us dwell a moment on the proposition in which so much passion is invested today: man is the being who possesses rights. It resonates as *our* self-definition and our perspective on humanity, one that we take to have fortunately replaced other definitions and perspectives, such as that man is God's creature or that man is a political animal. This definition certainly has assumed the authority from which other definitions used to benefit. It is not, however, of the same type. Not only is its content of course different, but it is also different *as a definition*, or in its form of definition. I think this will become clear if we compare it to the definition proposed by Aristotle: man is a political animal.

Aristotle's definition seems just as general, just as "abstract," as ours, but in fact it is of a very different type. Albeit indeed abstract, it "contains," as it were, all the concrete modalities of the most significant human competence, the one most proper to man, which it designates as the "political" competence. Positing that human beings organize their practical life in the best way by governing themselves in associations of a certain kind called "cities," it leaves it up to them, one might say, to put this capacity to work according to certain concrete modalities with their corresponding preferences, modalities that political science distinguishes and describes, thus developing and justifying this definition. As soon as we formulate this definition, as we still do readily today, our mind is filled with concrete images that evoke more or less clearly the political life of human beings, or their life in cities. Whatever may be the city, or even some other kind of human association, it is implicitly contained in this definition.

The elusive enigma of the definition that we are trying to grasp is something else entirely. As we have said, human rights, however we may render them explicit, presuppose a human world *already ordered* not by rights but by laws—political and moral laws, but also customary rules, such, for example, as those that guide the expression of sexual desire. They presuppose that the city and its diverse laws are *already there.* As we formulate our definition, what comes to mind are not concrete images of a human world *defined by* rights, but concrete images of "the struggle for rights," that is, of social movements or changes that, however important or desirable one judges them to be, intervene in an already constituted human world, such that our definition, unlike Aristotle's, is deliberately partial and biased. Moreover, in order for the form of our definition to be adequate to the idea or to the representation that it evokes, it would have to be modified as follows: human beings always and everywhere have the right to claim or to demand human rights. The only concrete or practical determination of these abstract rights is in effect that they are always and everywhere liable to be claimed by the subjects of these rights—that is, human beings—which distinguishes them radically from what today are called "animal rights." Even with this modification, this definition leaves the positive features of the human world, the world in which the human being has the right to claim human rights, in complete indeterminacy. There is no way to know, in particular, whether "the being with rights" is or is not a "political animal." Thus, whether we define the human being as "the being with rights" or as "having always and everywhere the right to claim human rights," we say *nothing* concerning what *constitutes* or *gives form to* human life.

The truth is that *nothingness* haunts this definition. We would not doubt this if we took seriously the approach of the founders of modern natural right. We take pleasure in comparing their various versions of the state of nature or of the social contract, and we question the status of their "hypothesis"; we evaluate, along with the coherence of their doctrines, their political or social relevance, or we go further and study the "context" of the elaboration of these teachings.

All that is very well, but if we stop there, there is a decisive element that escapes us, the very element that Thomas Hobbes puts before our eyes when he proposes to consider society or the city *tanquam dissoluta*—as if it had been dissolved or reduced to its elements—in order then to recompose it in a more rational manner. What is at stake here is more than a "question of method." We suppose that it is possible to reduce the human world to a kind of "degree zero," to nothing or almost nothing, to dismember it entirely in order then to reconstruct or recompose it entirely. We suppose that a human being can operate beginning with nothing, precisely with the nothing of humanity. I am by no means exaggerating, since, in speaking of man in the state of nature, Rousseau declares without qualification: "Limited to physical instinct alone, he is nothing, he is an animal."[7] To propose to think the human world by beginning with a human being from which the human has been "methodically" removed, in order finally to organize the world with justice and humanity, is an ambition or an enterprise that is at once exorbitant and affected by an "original vice."

One might reply that all that is "a thought experiment," that it is proposed "theoretically," or as a "hypothesis." To be sure—but this is a thought, theory, or hypothesis that is aimed at and orients or guides future action. In any case, what does it mean to think about such a matter? Perhaps to think our humanity does not fit so well with certain magical tricks: with what virtuosity our authors make "man" disappear and then reappear! One would have to admit that thought is capable of focusing on *what does not exist* or on *what is losing its being and its form*—more precisely, on a human world that is decomposing to the point of losing its human features, to the point of becoming a lawless condition in which human life, deprived of rules, no longer has anything human about it. The idea that the human mind could fix its attention on a condition in which all human traits are absent, or rather from which it must implacably remove all human traits while continuing to recognize the humanity of this condition, is a "hypothesis" that cannot be seriously considered, one that—with all due respect to the great minds who have wished to follow this path— involves an unpardonable element of frivolousness.

Of course it is possible to think "wound" without bleeding and to think "to kill" without being a murderer, but it is treating the effort of human thought lightly to imagine that we might effectively conceive and carry out a kind of "de-creation-re-creation" of humanity without experiencing a mortal upheaval. It is a fact that the thinker who went the furthest in this enterprise, who committed himself to it with the most depth and sincerity, was only able to follow through on it by according to himself the status and the prerogatives of the standard of the natural man, or of man according to nature. Rousseau was able to go so far in the deconstruction-reconstruction of man's humanity only because he believed he had found in himself the human being molded by nature itself and that this self-knowledge made possible the most precise knowledge of human nature as such. However, since we have contemptuously dismissed the very idea of a human nature, what is left that could possibly give life and being to this individual entitled to rights, that could give *human form* to this *conatus*, this unknown, this *x*? For us there remains *nothing*.

Let us go further. By conceiving, or claiming to conceive, a dissolution of the human city prior to its recomposition according to the best principles, we postulate a "power to think" or a "power to understand" that is essentially indifferent to and thus essentially superior to what it claims to think or to understand. It is as if the human intellect, the faculty of understanding, were comparable to a beam of light, a flashlight that can be pointed indifferently at a house in ruins or at a resplendent palace. This supposition may be pertinent or defensible where the understanding of nonhuman nature is concerned, since this nature obeys, at least largely, an observable and verifiable causality; but it is essentially unsuitable for understanding the human world, which is first of all a *practical* world, a certain *organization of action*, a certain *operation*. It cannot be approached judiciously without first drawing from this very world, from the human world *such as it appears*, the relevant information on the way action is organized within it, that is, without first being attentive to the way in which it understands itself. One may then, if there are good reasons for it, build a "better regime" in speech or in thought, but this is something very different from claiming to build the just city or the good society starting from this degree zero of humanity that is the state of nature or the *civitas dissoluta*—from separated individuals who are supposedly entitled to their rights.

This is why Socratic political science, the political science that Aristotle presents as the specific science of the human world, proceeds from a description of the way human cities *define themselves* in their own eyes, that is, first, the way they *understand themselves* and *speak of themselves*, thus starting with the opinions of citizens concerning their city. If we do not take seriously the diverse and sometimes opposing ideas of the just held by citizens, we disqualify ourselves from really understanding what goes on in the city, and thus from possibly elaborating a better city. I just evoked the way human cities *define themselves* in their own eyes. I would like in fact to emphasize that the object of practical science is *active*, that it takes a form in which the mind has its part, that it is inscribed in being in a way that excludes the knowing intellect's power to use it as it will, for example by subjecting it to a resolutive-compositive method that treats it like an object as devoid of speech as it is of thought. The truth is that, in order to achieve an adequate understanding of human cities, these must be considered as realities that speak and that think, and that might *cry out*. On the other hand, if one chooses to work with the formless inhabitant of the state of nature, whose poverty Rousseau recounted to us, then one is a *maker* who meets little resistance on the part of his *matter*—his prime matter—to use Hobbes's very terms. It follows that the work that is thought and projected is far from being a better city; it is not even a city, but a new institution that is not properly political, what the moderns call the state. Modern natural right does not properly found a political philosophy, but a doctrine of the state.

The Christian Question

The question then arises why such a way of thinking and such an institution developed in a Europe steeped in classical thought, a Europe that was, moreover, rich in diverse principles of action, including of course the Christian religion with its unheard-of propositions and the particularly strict demands it addressed to human beings. I will consider the question of Christianity, or of Christianity as a political question, only from the epistemological angle that interests us here, that of social knowledge and political science. The Christian religion presents a singularly resistant obstacle to Socratic political philosophy or to Aristotelian political science. The human condition announced and illuminated by Christianity, the condition of the *creature*, is still more rigorously determinate than the *political* condition experienced by the Greek city and analyzed by Greek political science. The creaturely condition is experienced and presents itself to the understanding as "enslavement to sin." All other components of the human world are subordinated to this fact, a fact that is controlling in an unprecedented sense. All powers of the human being are affected by this disorder in one way or another. It is thus a question of an enslavement that is insurmountable by man reduced to his own strength. Only Christ's grace can deliver him, the first step of liberation consisting in his becoming aware of the slavery of sin. The experience of sin and of grace is eminently decisive as well as strictly invisible: it operates *in foro interno*, in such a way that there is an essential difference—as it were, an essential incommunicability, between political experience and Christian experience. The citizen is visible and active in the midst of his fellow citizens, while the Christian takes his bearings by the invisible action of an invisible being infinitely different from himself, even though the Christian normally belongs to a visible ecclesial institution that guides his relation to God in a more or less detailed and rigorous way.

Therefore (limiting ourselves here to the problem of the *knowledge* of the human world) anyone who wishes to describe life in a Christian community under the regime of Christianity in the manner of Aristotle—that is, by starting with citizens' opinions on the just city or justice in the city—is confronted with a difficulty that will prove to be insurmountable. Shall he consider the dispositions and opinions of the citizen, or the dispositions and the faith of the Christian? The ambitions of the *agent*, or the reflections of the *penitent*?

He cannot look in the same way at the visible citizen and the invisible Christian, nor can he ask them to submit to the same kind of attention. What words will he trust: those that most faithfully manifest the city's opinions, those of the citizen who is always so sure of the justice of his claims, or those of the Christian, who is preoccupied first of all with his own injustice? This does not mean, moreover, that Christians inhabit only the regions of interiority. It is obvious that religions in general are the source of convictions and of passions that intervene visibly in the public space no less than political opinions and passions. Still, in the case of Christianity, however public, potentially influential, or even tyrannical the manifestations of the ecclesial institution may be, and however visible and audible may be the convictions of certain sectors at least of the Christian public, the center of gravity of Christianity resides in an interiority that no visible reality can reach and that no visible expression can express in a non-equivocal manner, given that the effect and the interior meaning of even the most public sacraments are inaccessible to the observer. It follows that behind the fabric of society an immense domain extends of which the invisible part is incomparably more significant and "real" than the visible part, thus a domain that cannot be mapped by any human instrument, by empirical observation or social science. In brief, under a Christian regime, the social *phenomenon* is at once overburdened and elusive. One might say that the intelligible surface of Christianity is impossible to "fix" because of the overabundance and equivocal character of its signs.

Over a long history many more or less judicious and durable accommodations have been made, and many mediations have been introduced between the political operation and the Christian operation,[8] the first of these being the Catholic Church itself. No one needs to be reminded that at a certain moment in our history this mediation came to appear unjustifiable or untenable to a "critical mass" of Europeans. What interests us here is not the practical and political failure of this mediation but what it means for social *knowledge*. When human life is divided between two operations of great power and depth, operations that are essentially independent of each other, it does not produce itself in the form of a synthetic phenomenon that can be taken into view to form the basis of an adequate political science. As damaging as it was, the disdain of the dogmatists of modern natural right for the social and political phenomenon can be said to have been inevitable, since it resulted from the overdetermination, or simply from the division or confusion, of the phenomenon itself. This division required an entirely new approach that was entirely detached from concern for the phenomenon, whether in its political or in its Christian version.

To get around this overdetermination or confusion of the human phenomenon, some resigned themselves or resolved to imagine and to produce a new basis of possible human determinations, or an indeterminate basis of humanity, whose law of construction demanded that it be emptied of political as well as of Christian determination—a basis of humanity on which to build a human world that would bring to light neither the political nor the Christian phenomenon, and thus one in which the political operation as well as the Christian operation would be in principle impossible, at least in their complete forms. Not being a citizen, this indeterminate basis of human rights would not be an agent in the proper sense; he would situate himself in the human world without knowing any rule of action; he would decide to ignore the fact that there cannot be action without a rule of action. Not being a Christian, he would not be reflective in the proper sense; he would situate himself in the human world without encountering a condemning law, able to see himself only as an *innocent*. The effort of modern natural right and of the state that it has inspired and informed was to bring to light this being defined by a right to be and to do that would be limited or ordered neither by the law of the city nor by the law of conscience.

The Meaning of the State

If the arguments I have just developed have some validity, then this means that the doctrines of modern natural right are based on mental constructions—the state of nature, human rights—that, far from being especially pertinent for guiding action and ordering the political body, tend rather to throw the rule of action into indeterminacy and to obscure more and more the sources of common life. To these arguments that target the intrinsic validity or logical consistency of a human right supposed to be prior to all law, the reader of Hobbes, or the observer of the modern state, or simply the practical person will oppose a counterargument that is not without force. I would sum up this argument as follows: Whatever the defects or obscurities of the notions or the mental constructions of modern natural right, the political meaning of the approach that they underlie is clear enough and in itself of great practical relevance. The point for members of society, for the subjects of sovereignty, in brief for all those who obey, is that they grant the sovereign, the one who commands, the quantity of power that that person needs in order to fulfill his function such as his subjects conceive it, that is, to protect them by repressing the ambitious or the factious who wish to dominate or exploit them. It is not hard to see in the theoretician's approach the outline, very vigorously drawn, of the construction of a political apparatus strong enough to repress the desire for superiority and to establish subjects or citizens on an equal plane, of which this apparatus is the protector and the guarantor. Whatever may be the philosophical weaknesses of the contractualist argument, the practical basis of the process envisioned is clear enough: it is the common interest—common up to a certain point—between the powerless many and the one who holds power.

This objection has a point. It rightly reminds us that the modern state was built against the enemy common to the many and the one, that is, the "few" in its many versions, not only the "nobles" or the "aristocrats" but also all intermediate bodies or mediators, including particularly the singular mediator that is the Catholic Church. This argument nevertheless leaves aside a practical question of great importance, that of the motives of action or the purposes proper to the bearer of sovereignty as an *agent*—a question that Hobbes omits entirely, since in his system, the sovereign, the holder of the greatest power humanly conceivable, has *no motive of his own* to exercise this sovereignty, receiving it as he does simply through its being abandoned or transferred from the *jus in omnia* of the subjects. The objective of the sovereign cannot be reduced to the domestication of the few, whatever importance this objective has taken on in the development of the modern state. Nor is it sufficient to object, as did Locke, that the subjects instructed by Hobbes imprudently nourish a lion or a tiger in order to protect themselves from foxes. The forgotten question is that of the motives proper to this lion or tiger, the motives proper to *the one who commands*, that is, who acts in the most complete sense or who alone carries out a complete action. The implicit argument that the one who commands "has an interest" in repressing those who would command is not sufficient. For if those who would command are moved by pride, how is it that the one who commands would not also be so moved, or moved even more by pride? Or how could the one who superlatively frightens others himself entirely escape fear? Hobbes's indifference to the motives of the one or the ones who command is justified only if the functioning of the political apparatus is essentially independent of the motives of those who control it—if the state produces its salutary effects independent of the government.

Moreover, while Hobbes takes account only of the motives of those who obey, he attributes to them only those that fit: since those who obey are constrained and dominated by fear, their motives are reduced to the desire to persevere in being in the most comfortable way possible. Machiavelli was more generous; he granted people a specific desire not to be oppressed, a motive that involves a certain intrinsic decency.[9] As I have already pointed out, from the point of view of the builder of the state, the human world does not find the basis of its ordered movement in the question What is to be done? This world is supposed to find its limits and be held together by the polarity between those who obey because they cannot, so to speak, do anything and those who command because they can, so to speak, do anything. But one who can do nothing does not act, does not even obey in the proper sense. Neither does one who can do anything act or even command in the proper sense. Since, in the new collective order, no one acts in the proper sense, then there is no point being concerned with the internal rule of action.

The Practical Question

How can the builder of the state forget or dodge so completely the *practical question* that subdivides into two distinct but inseparable questions, the *question of commanding* and the *question of the internal rule of action*? He forgets or dodges it as we have subsequently forgotten or dodged it, by granting to the proposition according to which all human beings are born and remain free and equal in rights the value of a founding axiom. If human beings are naturally free and equal, that means that obedience is *essentially* repugnant to them, that they are *essentially* recalcitrant. If obedience is essentially repugnant to them, if they are essentially recalcitrant, then the question of obedience becomes primary; it becomes the main political question—as it were, the only political question: the new and true political science, Hobbes insists, is a *science of obedience*.[10] How then are we to make people obey who are essentially recalcitrant, people who find in themselves no *reason* to obey? This is to ask at the same time how to produce the *power* capable of making them obey and how to make this obedience *just* or legitimate, that is, equal.

Leo Strauss maintained the thesis that modern political philosophy lowered the criteria of justice in order to make their application more certain and, so to speak, irresistible. It was from a starting point in his profound study of Hobbes's political philosophy that Strauss formulated this axial theme in his interpretation of modern political philosophy and, more generally, of the modern project or movement.[11] This thesis is at once suggestive and penetrating, but I will nevertheless criticize it as follows: it tends to obscure the immense indeterminacy that affects the instrument—that is, the sovereign state—by which the thus lowered criteria of justice are supposed to be applied. Criteria and application, justice and power—there we can agree. The state is in fact charged with bringing together power and justice, irresistible power and equal justice, but what remains indeterminate is *the morality proper to the state*, that is, the intention or the disposition by which it beats down the pride or represses the disobedience of subjects or of citizens. If we are condemned to ignorance concerning this intention, if it remains necessarily indeterminate, this is because the state draws its motivation, or rather its raison d'être and its basis, from the perspective of those who obey, not those who command. Those for whom obedience is essentially repugnant conceive and produce the instrument that will force them irresistibly to obey—the instrument that makes them obey in order then to obey them. Thus this immense apparatus, this *martellus infinitus*, does not know whether it is obeying or commanding, and the people who make use of it do not know either. This indeterminacy that combines opacity and duplicity indicates, more than any other characteristic, the vice of the modern state, the weakness that is intrinsic to its construction and the underside of its immense power.

In the moral penumbra of the state, the citizen unlearns what it is to obey and even more what it is to command. He unlearns together the two modalities of human action, particularly the main modality, that of commanding. The dominance of the state is the cause of an ongoing withering of human action and, at the same time, inseparably, of the growing obscurity of our understanding of action.

It is tempting to try to imagine the end point of the process of subjecting the political and social order to the state, the ultimate effect of this enigmatic institution that, wanting to be at once absolute sovereign and docile instrument, neither really commands nor obeys. The state commands with no specific reason all those who would like to command for any reason whatsoever. The state represses or contains those who would claim to command without itself pretending positively to command, even while officially declining to command itself, since it leaves free and equal citizens with their freedom. The immense machine of the state is busy emptying the social world of all commandment, busy producing a world without commandment, or with no other commandment than that of the state, which does not command in the proper sense—busy producing a human world in which no one either commands or obeys, in which each person is, as it were, reduced to the condition prior to action, a condition in which there is no rule available for guiding or concretizing action, such a rule being the condition of the distinction between one who commands and one who obeys. Commanding in fact has meaning in the human world only because he who commands or who claims to command discerns more clearly or takes his bearings more resolutely by the rule of action than those who are then led to obey are capable of doing. It is ultimately this rule of action that the great machine ceaselessly brings down, humiliates, and finally effaces as far as it is possible to do.

Thus, under the pressure of the state, the human being is reduced to the condition prior to action, or, as we have said using a word whose vacuity designates exactly the empty form that is thus produced, the condition of the "individual." The individual is defined abstractly as the being with rights and experiences himself concretely in the self's body as suffering or enjoying, in the *passivity* of the self's body as suffering or enjoying. Thus the modern state rests on a natural right that is posited and produced by the state, a right to which "modern" or "democratic society" conforms more and more in proportion to the deployment of the state. At the end of its course the modern state produces a social state that asymptotically approaches the state of nature as presupposed in its construction. The human being that will be called "modern" or "democratic" posits and produces himself according to a norm that has the authority of nature—human beings are born and remain free and equal in rights—but a nature posited and produced by the most powerful artifice ever conceived and constructed by human beings.

FOUR

The Law, Slave to Rights

Modern political science is a science of the state; at the same time it is, inseparably, a science of obedience. The state is the apparatus that irresistibly produces obedience, that irresistibly forces members of society to obey. As I have emphasized, this definition of the state has its underside, what one might call its corresponding "undefinition." This state, which causes obedience, does not command in the proper sense. At least we know of no principles that would motivate or illuminate its commands or of any positive purposes that it might pursue. More precisely, we do not know what kind of peace it imposes, what internal meaning it gives the external order that it guarantees with an unprecedented effectiveness and completeness. The question then arises: Given that members of society obey, whom or what do they actually obey? The instrumentality of the state confronts us, in a way, with an obedience without command, or an obedience whose link with commanding is in some way essentially indeterminate. Does it still make sense to speak of obedience? I have already mentioned the terms by which Thomas Hobbes provides us, if not with the true name of this obedience, at least with the principle that gives it meaning, that is, *authorization*: the sovereign's actions are *authorized* by those who obey and who are the true *authors* of these actions. Whatever he who commands me by the instrument of the state may do, I must acknowledge his actions as my own, since I authorized him to do what he would judge best to do as sovereign. As we know, this authorization is not as unlimited as it seems. In effect, although I have no right to disobey, since I regard the actions and decisions of the sovereign as my own, I can nonetheless resist or seek to escape from him if he attempts to take my life or to put me in a situation where I risk losing it: since the desire not to die at another's hands is the foundation of my obedience, I can without injustice refuse to obey orders that would put my life in danger. The admirable architect's plan that Hobbes has conceived and outlined is spoiled by some troubling points of fuzziness, even some large ink stains, in the places where the foundations of the edifice are supposed to be.

Thus, in the system of the modern state, one can no more speak properly of commanding than one can speak properly of obeying. How can one say that the subject or the citizen obeys, since in reality he authorizes, just as we do in our representative regimes, if not every day then at least on election days, when the subject or citizen stands at the beginning and at the source of the processes that produce the public organization of our representative regimes—and since, moreover, he can dispense with obeying whenever obedience would risk putting his life in danger, a risk from which we removed ourselves with palpable relief when we abolished conscription, authorizing the sovereign to put the citizen's life in danger only when the citizen is a volunteer, a "professional soldier"? What a strange system! How can this be understood, how can its mystery be unraveled? If, in this system, no one commands properly speaking and no one obeys properly speaking, this is because commanding has been separated from beginning. The *archē*[1] has been dismembered. This is the heart of the operation of the state.

The "Autonomous" Subject

Before further analyzing this dismemberment of which the modern state is at once the producer and the product, and in order to bring out its crucial significance, I would like to suggest that it has summoned the apparition of a specter that will continue to haunt not only our collective order but our intimate awareness of ourselves, the specter of the subject that commands itself, the specter of the *autonomous* subject. Recall that this is a notion that has no meaning in the classical understanding of human action and that for this reason was explicitly dismissed as a chimera conceived by the demon of analogy—in the event, by the analogy between the individual agent and the political body.[2] It was only owing to a growing incomprehension of the role and of the meaning of the pair of terms "command-obey" in practical life that this notion has had any plausibility; and the graver this obfuscation became, the more the specter grew in scope and authority, until it came to cover the poor agents that we have become with its boundless, albeit vain, pretentions.

To reduce the argument to what is essential, I would say something along the following lines. However bound together they may be, to command and to obey are two qualitatively different actions that therefore require different agents who stand differently in relation to the action. Each is complete as an action, and, I might say, each completely occupies the agent whether he is commanding or obeying. The agent who commands has no place in himself for one who obeys; the agent who obeys has no place in himself for one who commands. Let us have a closer look. He who commands *begins* the action. Once engaged, this action has the qualities included in its character as beginning-commanding. As a command it is a complete action and is assessed as such: has the agent commanded well? As for the action of the one who obeys, its character is that of an action that does not begin but only extends or pursues more or less faithfully: this is a case of a lesser action, an action, one might say, of lesser substance as an action; it is thus a *different* action, but as an act of obedience it is also a complete action. And it is assessed as such: has the agent obeyed well? Since it is a different action, there is no question of an agent being able to be in the position of commanding and of obeying with respect to *the same* action, of possessing at the same time and with respect to the same action the commanding and the obeying disposition. Once again, to command and to obey are two essentially different and equally complete actions. From the moment I try seriously to imagine that I am commanding myself or that I am obeying myself, I must imagine that the one who commands and the one who obeys are really two, and thus that I am obeying or commanding not myself, but someone other than myself, that is, *another*. I can imagine myself autonomous only by producing a *hetero*nomy within myself. In reality the agent as such is neither autonomous nor heteronomous, though he may be commanding or obeying. Autonomy and heteronomy are abstract notions that cover far too much to allow us to analyze the grammar of action with precision, and any plausibility we can accord them resides in their polarity, which translates or betrays abstractly the concrete polarity between commanding and obeying.

The argument that I have just presented in a summary way might well call forth the following objection, one that seems to have some common sense in its favor: Can I not *command myself* to stop smoking or to overcome my fear of spiders, or even a more fearsome enemy? Are not commands of this type at the origin of the "victories over ourselves"—too rare, alas—that make us "content with ourselves" and win the compliments of those close to us? Here we must beware of a confusion. A person can indeed command himself to stop smoking. This command is also a beginning, and we are indeed dealing here with a full and complete action since it has its reasons, or it is not without reason: one stops smoking for reasons of health (one's own or that of others who are close); or to save money, since tobacco has become quite expensive; or to be free of an addiction, and so on. Still, although the one who commands indeed appears in this act, this is not the case concerning the one who obeys, since "the one who obeys" is only *a part* of the one who commands—his body, his passions, or his bad habits. As I said above, to obey is truly an action, that is, a complete action. Now, to make the recalcitrant parts of our being obey in no way opens up the space for such an action. When I exercise this power of commanding, I am the one who commands; I am not the one who obeys, since *the one* who obeys simply does not exist.

"To stop smoking," like the other "victories" of this kind, belongs to what the tradition called the power of the soul over the body or simply "self-mastery," the acquisition of which once made up a principal part of education. The idea of autonomy has practically nothing to do with that of self-mastery. As a matter of fact, the idea of autonomy gained the authority it has today only insofar as the idea of the power of the soul over the body or of self-mastery has lost its own. The two ideas are mutually exclusive; they are opposed in the same way that a natural order, an "order of the soul" that is demonstrated and affirmed in self-mastery, is opposed to one that is anything but natural since it is, on the contrary, supposed to be produced by the subject itself in the operation by which it is supposed to command itself and obey itself. Since it is law that is the source of commanding as well as of obeying, to command, in the order of autonomy, is to produce the law, and to obey is to obey the law thus produced. This is why, as was summed up in the passage from Thomas Aquinas cited above, according to classical moral philosophy, one could speak of autonomy only with reference to a political body, the only possible context for "giving oneself the law." "To stop smoking" thus belongs to the old order of self-mastery and in no way to the new order of autonomy.[3]

As I have said, the loss of concrete understanding of the qualitative difference between commanding and obeying and the obfuscation or oblivion of the phenomenon of commanding and thus also of that of obeying result from or prepare the system of the state. Founded on an authorization that is neither command nor obedience but envelops the confusion of the two, the state obliges members of society to live in a social-political world in which neither commanding nor obeying is any longer clearly visible, since they no longer exist in the integrity of their concrete polarity. The apparently, or rather conspicuously, extreme character of obeying as well as commanding in the regime of sovereignty conceived by Hobbes cannot mask the secret evisceration that both undergo. Under cover of this double parody, the great machine of the state shelters a member of society who obeys just as little as the state commands him, or who, more precisely, rather than obeying the state that commands him, adopts more and more a manner of conduct that resembles obeying in order to comply with state rules that look like commands. The member cannot properly obey these commandments from the state that are not commandments, but he fits more and more *the mold of the state*, this general disposition to let himself be shaped, a disposition that is not really obedience since it never encounters a sincere and complete act of commanding. Having been molded by the state, set up in this opaque condition where mutilated and confused notions of commanding as well as of obeying blend together, the member of society takes on a form by, and takes pride in, seeing himself as one who gives himself commandments, who obeys himself, an illusion or chimera that experience cannot dissipate because the state system protects this member from any actual encounter with either commanding or obeying. The more he is shaped by the state and becomes incapable of commanding as well as obeying, and, moreover, of understanding what it means to command and to obey, the more he sees himself as self-commanding and obeying himself, then the more he situates himself and prides himself on this imaginary condition, that of a subject or an autonomous individual, an unrecognized but faithful product of the unperceived tyranny of the state.

The Law against Itself

In the modern natural-right teaching as in the state system, as I was just saying, commanding and obeying tend to lose their meaning and their proper substance. It is of course the fate of commanding that is determinant, while that of obeying is only a consequence. Commanding is in effect the eminent or excellent modality of action, for the very simple reason that action itself, action as such, includes an intrinsic component of commanding or is based or hinges on a pivot-point of commanding. This pivot-point of commanding is the rule or the reason of action—the rule or the reason without which action would not even come to awareness and without which of course there would be no question either of deliberation or of decision. The rule of action is no less "commanding" when the agent disdains to take account of it, dismisses it, or goes against it. Thus there are commands and commanding agents, in this world or in the other, only because action and the human agent are naturally and necessarily under the rule of action. The most brutal and blind tyrant draws the possibility of his being, one can say, from reason's command, which he ignores, but which is implicit in practical life as such, a command that is concretized in the rules proper to diverse actions or categories of actions.

The error of modern natural right, an irreparable error, even an unpardonable error, because it presupposes a willing blindness, resides in the idea that it is possible to produce the command starting from a condition of noncommand, from a state of nature or of natural freedom, which would know nothing of command. The point is not only that one would seek in vain where the idea of command could possibly come from in a world that knew nothing of it,[4] or how to establish it "by convention" without first having the "natural" experience of it. This, to put it more directly, is because the necessity and the legitimacy of commanding are given with the very constitution of the human world as a practical world, a world of action, a world that presupposes in its mere intelligibility that action has reasons that in principle govern it, reasons that the human agent often ignores or distorts, but without which he would be incapable even of choosing his perversity or his dissidence, which would have neither meaning nor appeal. It is the human agent's clearer and deeper understanding of the reasons of action that allow him to introduce more order and reason in the part of the human world that is within his competence, whether he is a skillful negotiator, an audacious strategist, a wise politician, or a discerning spiritual director; and it is by his personal command that he gives effect to reason's natural command.

Thus, on the one hand, there is no natural freedom, there is no human condition without command; and on the other hand, the practical world is never given over essentially to the arbitrary commands of gods or of human beings, because along with action come the reasons for action and because the human agent cannot engage in action without entering to some degree into its reasons. There is so much disorder in the world, and the unreason of human beings is so plain to see, only because the human world is essentially albeit potentially ordered, because it is only thinkable or livable by these rules and reasons that give meaning to human actions, however human beings may follow them, which is often quite badly.

It is within such a world, a world essentially albeit potentially ordered, that political law intervenes as the principal ordering authority, the potential cause of the most salutary order as well as of the most devastating disorder. Political law—the law that *governs*—places itself at the summit of practical life, as does the sovereign state, but with this difference, that political law finds its place *within* the practical order, without whose resources it would not know what cardinal point to aim at, as inept as the Leviathan that has all power but no idea which way is north. It situates itself within the order of practical life, an order that, as we have emphasized, is governed by the pair "command-obey" according to the indications or orientations given by the rule of action as refracted in the diversity of its domains and modalities, from contract law to medical ethics to penal justice. Precisely because this order of practical life is ordered and animated by all kinds of disparate rules and reasons—there are also rules on how to properly tie one's necktie, or "to sway the festoon and the hem"[5]— and because the goods at which our actions aim are of very unequal quality and often incomparable or even incompatible, it is indispensable that this teeming and mobile architecture be held together, united, and crowned by a keystone that is at once weighty, protective, and animating, the political law, the law that *governs*. This law dominates the practical world—otherwise it could not govern—it is *kurios*, or *kuria*,[6] but it exists and has meaning only because *there is* a practical world.

Political law has two characteristics: on the one hand, it gives the main directives intended to guide this practical whole, this practical operation, constituted by every political community; on the other, it has the right and the power to repress by force all contravention of its commands, which are assumed to be fully legitimate unless challenged before a constitutional tribunal, according to the diversity of institutions that is not our subject here. Political law is thus *at once* directive and constraining, and the conjunction of these two traits accords it the specificity and the eminence that characterize it. At the same time, all rules of action in the human world possess these two traits to some degree. The deontology of a profession includes both certain directives and certain variable modalities of constraint, which range from censure to professional exclusion, a "bad reputation" being not a minor punishment. Although on the one hand political law or government is the summit of the practical order, albeit only the summit, on the other—that is, at the most modest echelons of the practical order—certain seeds of government are present and active: even the agent who is most detached from all association and dispensed from following the least communal rule—imagine for the moment such a possible case—would nonetheless be "subject to the rule" because he would always have to pose the question What is to be done?—and because this question not only would have no answer but would have no meaning if it could not be illuminated by a rule of action, however difficult to find and still more difficult to apply such a rule might sometimes be. If we examined the practical association from bottom to top and in every direction, without neglecting any corner or hidden stairway, we would not find an individual left to his natural freedom or simply enjoying this freedom and the rights that supposedly go with it. One might be without a country, which is not an enviable condition, or perhaps homeless, but one cannot be without law or rule, because that would mean that one is not an acting being, and thus that one does not belong to humanity.

Thus, as I have emphasized, whereas the *practical and political* order involves a gradient connected by many ladders none of whose rungs is left practically indeterminate—that is, none is exempt from the rule of action and the polarity commanding-obeying that corresponds to this rule—the *statist* order is based on the polarity between two kinds of indeterminacy: the indeterminacy of a social life that tends toward ever more freedom, ever more "new rights," and the indeterminacy borne by a sovereign state that possesses a monopoly on legitimate commands, commands whose indeterminacy we have emphasized. It follows that, while the state extends its empire over our practical and political life, the practical world, the world of rule-bound action, is in the grip of a scheme of ever more ruleless freedom at whose summit there is a sovereign whose principles of action are nevertheless more and more uncertain. The paradoxical status of the law in the modern scheme consists in the fact that it occupies the pole of the supreme rule of action, that it retains this role since a human order cannot subsist without a rule of action, and that at the same time it deploys its superiority and its command over a human world that knows nothing of or wants to ignore the practical order and has no place for any rule of action whatsoever, since it is determined originally and essentially as natural freedom or life without law. The modern state intends to rule a human world that believes itself or wishes itself to be without law or rule.

We have given this enterprise, hopeless but not without consequence, the advantageous appearance of a beneficial redefinition of the law, a redefinition that consists no longer in setting down the best rules or the best regime, but in guaranteeing and promoting the rights in which natural freedom consists. Henceforth the law proposes to give members of society only those commands necessary to lead a life without law. Everything that goes beyond this limit, that might have some positive content or aim at a definite good, a way of life judged to be good, is held in some way to violate human rights and to take us back into the old world of commanding and obeying. We want to replace a practical world consisting in actions regulated by all kinds of rules of varying amplitude, rigor and precision, according to more or less independent and always tangled gradients, with a world of simple polarity in which political law, now confused with state commands, has no meaning other than authorizing and no function other than organizing a life without law—what we call freedom. We have required political law to be something other than and finally contrary to a law; we have required *political* law to act against its essence as *law*, an essence from which it cannot, however, rid itself.

This is no doubt the deep cause of the specific opacity of modern society, an opacity that the sciences we call precisely "social" address and aim to overcome. Once modern society had taken up the viewpoint and, as it were, the mission of attaining the greatest possible freedom and the most extensive individual rights, and this by the methodical suppression of all commands or rules of action produced and borne by the collectivity, it demanded, in order to grasp itself or rather to grasp itself once again, that there be determinations of a new kind, no longer political or social commands that each person can perceive but "social causes" discernible only by specialized observers. The more the laws that are properly practical and political, laws and rules that command visibly, are weakened, the more difficult we find it to represent to ourselves the practical and political whole of which we are members, and the more we need to bring about a new modality of collective order, henceforth held together in our eyes by laws of another type, the "laws of society." While the "vertical" and visible commands were being effaced, there arose the "horizontal" sway of a new authority and, as it were, a new substance, the "society" that "commands" us in an unprecedented sense, by causing us to act in a certain way without our being able to escape its influence or even be aware of it without the light of a specific kind of knowledge.

There is no need here further to elaborate the social and intellectual movement that is one with the deployment of sociology along the arc that goes from Montesquieu to Durkheim. What must be noticed, however, is that in the most recent period the need or the hope of setting forth the laws of society, or, more generally, of understanding the social whole in its order and its movements, its statics and its dynamics, has withered or rather dissipated. Sociology, the royal science of society and of the modern world, has now largely renounced the ambition that constituted it. More precisely, rather than seeing in society a whole made up of objective forces incomparably more powerful than the individuals who believe themselves to be free, it now looks on institutions, along with the ideas that support them and give them meaning, as "social constructions" destined to practical and theoretical "deconstruction." Whereas in its origins sociology saw the individual with his subjective freedom as the product of the objective laws of the social body in its modern form, it now sees a limitless individual freedom coming to light victoriously against social stereotypes. Rather than correcting the illusions of the sovereign freedom of the individual, it delivers up social norms to the individual subjectivity, whose side it takes without reserve. It is as if the progress of freedom—that is, of practical indeterminacy—had discouraged the hope of achieving a theoretical determination of society as a whole rich with power and with meaning, unless this progress had relieved us of the need: established in a life without law, released from commands and rules, seeing in itself and around itself only individual rights to assert, why would the subject be concerned with looking for "laws of society" or for "social causes"—that is, for the sources of collective being—since in its eyes there is no longer a life in common. The social sciences no longer have a "social fact" or a "social movement" to illuminate. Contrary to their raison d'être, today's social sciences assume the task of highlighting the unreality of society, thus only confirming the spontaneous feeling of dissociated members of society.

Political Law and Modern History

In these very summary remarks I have tried to bring to light the nerve of a political and scientific development of great magnitude, one of long duration and with contradictory manifestations. Focusing here on principles, I cannot give history, either political or intellectual, the place it deserves. I have just mentioned the recent disappearance of sociology as the ambition to understand this new object that was modern society, or simply *society* as such. The irruption of modern freedom, as I have just recalled, was soon accompanied by the elaboration of a new understanding of the collective order, no longer as commanded but as caused or necessitated. The abyss of political and social indeterminacy that had opened up found its correlate in an immense ambition of knowledge. The quest for theoretical certainty, for Science, responded to the practical vertigo. At the same time, the reconstruction of order was not left to the learned alone. Practical men, politicians and citizens themselves, not all readers of the sociologists, responded to the indeterminacy that had opened up with institutional constructions of great amplitude and ambition. A new political life was breathed into the statist order to which the dying ancien régime seemed to have given its final form. Even though the principles of natural freedom tended to separation, as Marx initially brought out and as we would later observe, it was in their name that the institutions of political liberty were built. By generalizing civil and political rights and by guaranteeing "public liberties," by organizing and giving life to the representative regime, even though in effect they substituted abstract procedures for concrete social "commands," the fathers of the republic enlarged the scope of practice and liberated the energy that made it possible to undertake an unprecedented political operation. I would characterize this operation as the pursuit of the rule of common action. What was the modern republic, in effect, in the period that might be called classical, if not *a common action in search of its rule*? Thus, in the first period of their implementation, the extension and the guarantee of abstract rights contributed to the concretization of a great political action. By disempowering or subverting established social and religious authorities, the democratic movement necessitated an ambitious reassumption and redefinition of the common.

It is difficult to determine the exact *point of inflection* at which the extension of rights, rather than giving the institution force and energy, and sometimes its very existence, began to strip it of its substance or to dilute this substance, and all the more difficult because this point of inflection did not appear at the same time in all the domains of collective life. We would not be too far from the truth, however, in situating this point or these points of inflection in the 1960s, or perhaps in a "1968 moment." In any case, beginning then, all the great institutions in succession, first the Catholic Church, then the university, and finally the nation, had to confront a radical contestation of their proper legitimacy and their internal meaning.

It was not only that their members manifested a more and more intense desire to loosen and eventually to eliminate the rules of these institutions. The movement came also from the outside, or rather it aimed to efface the boundary between the inside and the outside, between the church and the "world," between the university and society, between the nation and humanity. The unlimited sovereignty of individual rights became an unanswerable argument for anyone who wanted to prevail against the rules and the meaning of any institution whatsoever. In this way French legislators and judges, by rejecting the principle of selection in university admissions, tended to deprive what is doubtless the most useful and most just or the most noble institution produced or refounded by modern politics of its meaning and its substance. In this way, in the name of the principle of human rights, we want to prevent nations from passing laws that they might judge useful or necessary in order to preserve or encourage the common life and education that give each its physiognomy and its raison d'être. It is no longer up to political communities to determine who will be a citizen and under what conditions, since now each person is supposed to have the right to become a citizen of the state he or she chooses. Whatever the institution, one can say, every individual has the unconditional right to become a member—unconditional, that is, without having to be subject to the specific rules, to the "law" that governs the life of that institution, or by subjecting themselves only in the most approximative and, as it were, disdainful manner. Whether the question concerns the nation, the family, or the university, the institution is unable to oppose its rule to the individual who invokes his desire or his right, the two now being hard to distinguish. As I noted in the previous chapter, under the exclusive legitimacy of the principle of human rights, all aspects of the human world are delivered up to a *jus omnium in omnia*. Let us be clear here that this "right" is understood in a more and more extensive way, indeed in a way that is properly unlimited: not only as the right to "have it all" but, more troubling still, as *the right to be everything that we are or want to be.* How can this be?

The Right to Be All That We Want to Be

In order to be effectively recognized and guaranteed, this right must be determined by law, since law alone effectively organizes collective life. But how can we determine a right to be all that we are or want to be? How can it be given form or content? How can we determine, identify, verify, or merely guess what we are or want to be? The question for each individual is of course infinite. Fortunately, or unfortunately, the *right to be* has been declared and legalized before there has been any response to the question, or even any serious concern with responding to the question. Here it is much more important to have a right than to know what one has a right to. The decisive point to be noticed is that what we are or want to be *is not* what we do or want to *do*. What we do or want to do puts us immediately under the law, or under the rule of action, even when, as is the case today, the very idea of a law or a rule has been much weakened. We may well protest that our desire knows neither law nor rule, but once we carry out an action or undertake something practical, we are dealing with a rule. As a matter of fact, if we are doing or wish to do *something*, that presupposes that we could do or want to do *something else*. We cannot give an account of the choice we make, even in our own eyes, without reference to a rule, or rather in general to certain rules of diverse kinds and belonging to diverse registers. Every action and every plan of action confronts us with the question of the rule of the action and exposes us to the judgment of those close to us, of fellow citizens, or of our conscience: Is our action, or will our action be, courageous, just, prudent, moderate? To find ourselves under the law and exposed to judgment is what we refuse above all when we intend not only to have our rights respected but to *define ourselves* by our rights, rights whose whole meaning resides in the authorization that they demand and promise. The authorization of action does not include the rule of action, but it does not dispense us from seeking this rule. The authorization to do something, as extensive as it may be, does not deliver us from the law. In our frantic flight from law, in our principled refusal of law, we covet an authorization that would suffice unto itself, that would not require the complement of a personal search for the rule, however lazy or random our search might be. This is the point at which the right to be all that we are or want to be intervenes.

There is always a law. There is always the law. In order for the law to relieve us of the law, it is necessary and it suffices that, rather than guiding our action, it comes to concern or recognize our passion or our passivity. Once rights have reached the limit of their extension; once they have established their exclusive legitimacy by victoriously opposing all collective rule; once the law, slave to rights, has, as it were, no more "practical matter" to rule, it comes to seek out each person in his or her subjective suffering or enjoyment—*politically* these come to the same thing, for in both cases the individual is convoked in his passivity—and it brings this suffering or enjoying "I" into the public light, commanding all to recognize this suffering or enjoying—to "recognize," that is, to grant it a value that can be opposed to any law or rule whatsoever. Under this law of "recognition" (for the law still rules under the abolition of all rule), the human being ceases to be a political animal, a definition, as we have seen, that carries with it a whole swarm of eminently practical questions, of which the most penetrating inquire into the city's best regime or the just political order. The law of rights has no place for these questions. Under its power, the human being also ceases to be a rational animal confronted with the challenge of acting well, since reason is the commanding and legislating authority par excellence and the point of the law of rights is to strip all legitimacy from reason as commanding. Henceforth the human being, if he is still susceptible to definition, is a sentient or sensitive animal, an "I" qualified by the way he "feels" his life, or is "affected" by it, a closed circle of self-adhesion, a tautology of self-feeling from which no question proceeds and which can hear no question: the living-individual without either city or reason, ceaselessly busy reducing its being to what it feels of it and at the same time to gaining recognition for his being as he feels it.

Thus, by assuming as its unique mission the guarantee and assertion of the rights of the sentient and sensitive "I," the new law engages in the strange enterprise of bringing into the public light and establishing in the public light what naturally escapes or spontaneously flees this light. We have rejected with disgust or disdain the old law, the practical and commanding law, the law that claimed to rule the visible action of members of society in the various fields in which action was deployed; for us the old law is barbarism and tyranny. Henceforth the new law calls the secret feeling of the "I" to come into the daylight and to remain there under its protection—in brief, to perform its "coming out," the gesture that earns one celebration as a hero, as is appropriate since, by reversing the relationship of the private and the public, it signals and consecrates the power of the new law. As we see, the right declared and guaranteed by the new law does not concern the "part" or the "contribution" of each person to what is in common, but each individual's relationship to himself, divorced from all participation in the common life, or even deprived of all significance for the common life. The new law as protector of new rights by predilection reaches and illuminates a part of being that does not belong to the public domain, however this may be understood. The old law might well have "aimed at" this intimate part of the human being as it formulated its prohibitions, but, in repressing or reproving homosexuality, for example, it left it in the intimate domain where enjoyment naturally escapes the law. This is not to contest the unpleasantness, humiliations, and wounds involved in the old order. Nor do we contest that fact that the new law "improves the condition" of the concerned persons. Still it is notable that these new freedoms and new rights imply certain new constraints—first of all, for the persons concerned, whom the new laws paradoxically put once again under the law—under a law of authorization, to be sure, but an authorization that involves, if not the obligation, then at least an incentive to come out of the secret zone proper to private life. Is it not the case that to remain in secret, or merely discreet, is unjustly to disavow the law that cares for your rights? Next, there are constraints for the fellow citizens of the persons concerned, that is, for those who are obliged to know without the least ambiguity something they are not necessarily keen to know, as the new law summons them to prove that they find nothing to remark in what they are forced to notice. Thus the new law, a law of freedom and authorization, forces some to publish and others to take notice of and, as it were, to validate what the first would sometimes prefer to leave, if not in secret, at least in the penumbra that is natural to the passions, especially to those passions that the old law reproved, and that in no way are limited to homosexual passions.

While the law of prohibition—including under this term all that pushed homosexuality underground—repressed or held back the visible conduct of homosexuals, the law of authorization, by incentivizing them to make themselves visible, claims to rule over the feelings and judgments of their fellow citizens. The law of authorization is surely "milder" than the law of prohibition, but by taking on an unattainable objective—that is, to secure in a verifiable way the disappearance of feelings and judgments that are unfavorable or reserved with respect to homosexuality—this law is vulnerable to the inquisitorial drift that we have seen in our countries, in which every person is summoned to manifest in all possible ways that he has no "prejudices." We are forbidden to express, or even to let slip, the least reservation concerning the law of authorization, a law that carries offenses of opinion and crimes of heresy in its wake.

One's relation to oneself, the life of feelings, the orientation of desire, however one regards and judges these matters, are of no concern to the common life, in any case to political life. The sexual orientation of the agent, whether he is considered as a citizen or as a worker, does not affect his activity as a citizen or a worker; or, if it does affect it, this is in a way that interests only himself and that is of no concern to those who participate with him in a common action or enterprise. This separation of the intimate and the private from the common or the public is hindered when the relation to oneself, in its different modalities, is set up in public view, when it is, as it were, forced to occupy the public space. From this point on, in effect, the public space is less and less open to or available for the action and the institution that are as such indifferent to the subjects' "feeling of self." Action and institution hardly find support anymore in a social atmosphere saturated by the subjective claim of those who demand recognition not for what they do but for what they are. Social energy, rather than being spent mainly on "going beyond oneself," on entering into shared activities and participating in common life, is increasingly diverted to the assertion of the feeling, however incommunicable, of the living-individual, the sensate and sensitive "*I.*"

The Right to a Universal Income

Let us consider the idea of a universal guaranteed income in the light of this discussion. The popularity, durable although variable, of this idea is revelatory of a profound tendency of our social sensibility. Such an income would be entirely independent of all work, all activity, initiative, or contribution by the rights bearer, who has never better deserved the name than in this context. This income would be attached unconditionally to the fact of being alive, in order to make the continuation of life possible and to render it sufficiently pleasant. The immemorial torment, the deep pain of humanity exposed to the pressure of need and the burden of work, would come to an end; this ever-so-painful knot would finally be untied, since the collective order would give each person the possibility along with the authorization to live without working. Delivered from the necessity of work, life would be delivered from necessity itself.

The invincible need to persevere in being provided the foundation and the motivating force of modern natural rights, the idea of a power right—the power right of the *conatus*—that is valid and active independently of all law and all common concern. A universal income would liberate the right of the living-individual from his dependency in relation to the support of our animal nature, to the needs bound up with the life of the body. It would cut the root of human dependency in relation to an objective order of things. Thus humanity would, as it were, receive life from its own hand, devoting its last effort to establishing itself in the terminal passivity of a life not needing to be earned, a life that could be received without gratitude since everyone would receive only *what they had a right to.*

With the institution of a universal income, the modern state would achieve the limit of its extension by taking over its condition of possibility and mastering it. This immense edifice rested on the need of the living-individual. It drew its power and its authority from the urgent and imperious or irresistible character of the need of the living-individual, proposing itself as this individual's docile and omnipotent instrument. By distributing a universal income, the state delivers the living-individual from need. Thus arises the question, What basis and motive can henceforth support and animate the state?, since, by eliminating the principled dignity of work along with its necessity, the state deprives both itself and the life that it shelters of their foundation. Of course the universal income will not be established, and necessity will not be abolished. Still, by moving in this direction, by making a universal income the last frontier of what is desirable, we deprive humanity of its last serious reason, and of the specifically modern reason, for *acting*.

FIVE

The Individual and the Agent

The reader has doubtless been disappointed by the little place that I have accorded in the preceding chapters to arguments that might be said to be properly or specifically philosophical, and the reader may be surprised by the importance that the question of the state has taken on in my discussion. I hope to have provided some solid reasons to justify my approach. I would like in any case to summarize them here. On the one hand, the modern state is inconceivable without the philosophical elaboration that accompanied and guided its construction; it is inseparable from it. As I have said, modern political philosophy is mainly or, rather, essentially a philosophy of the state. We often fail to derive the consequences, or to appreciate the implications, of this widely shared or sharable observation. On the other hand, the political, moral, and social history of European humanity has been profoundly informed by the deployment of the state.

The state has changed our condition—according to the most favorable and most widely received interpretation, it has improved our condition—by changing the conditions of action. This expression indicates the enormity of the transformation undertaken. Since the human being in its most specific definition is the acting animal, the most decisive changes that may affect this being concern the conditions of action. It would certainly be a simplification, but I think an illuminating simplification, to say: Western humanity—that is, humanity understood as having entered into a history—has known two great changes, two revolutions, affecting the conditions of action. The first consisted in the crystallization of the city in Greece, the second in the construction of the modern state. These are the two revolutions that have most deeply affected the human being, that have most deeply transformed it. Between these two, the Christian religious revolution must surely be given its place. This revolution, for the first and only time in human history, proposed principles of action independent of all previously existing political association and capable by themselves of producing a human community of an unprecedented kind, that is, the church.

Whatever may be the case on this last point, the revolution of the state had for its objective and its effect the indefinite augmentation of the level or the degree of human activity by two inseparable approaches, or by a double approach that might be summarized thus: on the one hand, the equalization of the conditions of action; on the other, the limitation or circumscription of the amplitude or the range of action. These are therefore the three determining parameters of modern life under the revolution of the state: the augmentation or intensification of activity (which of course, and precisely, must not be confused with action), the equalization of the conditions of action, and the shrinking of its perimeter or of its ambition. It is difficult to rank these parameters or to attribute a leading role to one or another. We see clearly enough, moreover, how, among the different political or social movements, the different opinions that lead modern society on, certain ones are associated by predilection with the acceleration of the movement of human beings and of things, others with equality of conditions, and others still with the limitation of the actions of human beings on one another. In any case it is the coming together of these three vectors under the pressure and the direction of the state that gives the modern revolution its prodigious power to transform human life. The definition of man as the being with rights has plausibility only on the condition of an indefinite or "deregulated" human activity, or a human activity with no other rule than the equality of conditions at the start, or, as we now say, equality of opportunity, an equality which for its part demands that human beings avoid deploying capacities or competencies that might give some a superiority of legitimate command over others, not a simply functional superiority but an intrinsic and, as it were, "natural" superiority. In any case, this triple determination places the experience of modern life, and the idea we make of it, under a regime of constraints whose rigor we are prevented from feeling by a long habituation. These constraints weigh most particularly on the notion in which the moderns have placed their joy and their pride, that is, freedom.

It is stating a commonplace to say that for the moderns, the notion of natural law is indefensible and finally devoid of meaning, since it is incompatible with and even directly contrary to the definition of humanity as freedom, a definition that is of a piece with our self-consciousness as "subjects," or as "individuals," or precisely as "self-consciousness." Law can have meaning for human beings, at least for human beings who have attained this self-consciousness, only if it is a product or an expression of their freedom. How it is that the rational animal posits a law independent of and superior to any natural determination either of the individual or of the species is a question that opens an immense range of propositions and speculations. The prestige of these speculations, in which the specific audacity and profundity of modern philosophy are deployed, must not blind us to the fact that modern freedom, understood as a concrete proposition of the radical recomposition of our way of life by the methodical and complete transformation of the conditions of human action, came about along more prosaic paths and that, moreover, when these speculations were taking off, the decisions had already been made and the foundations already laid, decisions and foundations that were not to be reconsidered. It is important, in effect, not to forget that modern freedom was born as a fast friend of this nature that it would later come to treat or pretend to treat from such a position of superiority; it was born as an extension and need of this nature. More precisely, modern freedom was born as nature liberated, as nature unbound: freedom, for the moderns, is first of all the removal of impediments to nature.

That was true at the beginning, and it remains true at the end of the movement. What is sexual freedom, a freedom that is so central to the contemporary understanding of freedom that it tends to constitute the representative expression of that freedom and something like its critical experience—what is this freedom if not the suppression of all material, legal, and moral obstacles to the satisfaction of sexual desires? But these liberated or authorized desires cannot be characterized otherwise than as natural determinations of the living-individual, as we see in the insistence already noted on the fact that sexual orientation never or in any degree results from a person's choice. As enthusiastically as we generally invoke it, freedom here is in the service of natural necessities or tendencies, or in the service of a desiring nature that violently rejects any suggestion of a possible opening to freedom as reflective choice. Hence the glowing attention and the merit we see invested in the "coming out" that I evoked in the preceding chapter: to come out is the first and the last choice, it is the only choice, the only free act that is open to a person once he conceives himself as the living-individual subject to the necessity of his desire.

Laissez-Faire, Laissez-Passez

Although the movement of nature's liberation (for this is how the vector of modern freedom ought to be designated) takes ever-new forms, thus ever-surprising and even shocking forms, for contemporaries, the activating principles of this liberation are not only present and active but even explicit and even thematic from the time of its initial engagement. I have recalled from the outset the importance of the notion of *conatus*, which distills the original and principal modern determination of human nature. It is time to add that it is inseparably an essential ingredient of the modern idea of freedom. This effort to persevere in being, this beginning of movement, this desire for power, this desiring machine—the point is to liberate it, to remove the obstacles that oppose or hinder its deployment. In brief, *laissez-faire, laissez-passer*—this is the simple but prodigiously seductive formula of modern freedom, whether it is a question of the circulation of wheat, of workers, of ideas, or of drives.[1] There is always a part of society, a sector of activity, an aspect of human nature, or a domain of being that is still trammeled. There is always a new freedom and there are always some new rights to promulgate in order to remove restraints, to free up and liberate the natural necessity that was already there and making its pressure felt. This natural necessity reigns not only over our material and passionate nature; our very ideas are subject to it. One of the favorite arguments of the seventeenth and eighteenth centuries for rejecting the government of opinions by law can be summed up something like this: How can law, whether political or religious, legitimately command our opinions, when we do not have power over our own thoughts, the ability to think one thing rather than another, to believe or not to believe, for example and especially the power to believe that God does or does not exist? These commands and this censorship are illegitimate and unjust for the same reason that they are essentially powerless: they claim to do what it is impossible to do, to oblige us to *choose* what we think or believe. Modern freedom consists in liberating our natural necessity by dismissing the illusion of freedom—the illusion of free will, the illusion of free choice—that hides this necessity from us and justifies commands that are as oppressive as they are ineffective.

The argument that I have just recalled can be found in Hobbes as well as in Spinoza or Bayle. In fact, the most important or most influential philosophers in the elaboration of the liberal project are practically all resolute and explicit critics of the Greek conception of reflective choice as well as the Christian conception of free will and conscience. While it is certain that they want to liberate humanity from the shackles that hold them back and constrain them, it may be doubted that the human beings they want to liberate are agents capable of the complete practical operation that the Greeks thus called reflective choice and that the Christians called free action. For the fathers of liberalism, the decision that determines action is the last step in a process that is finally mechanical, a competitive process that gives the advantage to the strongest "preference," a process of which the individual is the site and the witness, but in which he does not intervene as a truly free agent.

To be sure, minds so well advised knew what they were doing. If they deprived human beings of their free will in order to liberate them, this is because the former action was the condition of the latter. "Freedom" could not be offered as the ultimate or main goal to a human being endowed with free will, an agent capable of reflective choice. However inconvenient, painful, and even humiliating may be obstacles external to his body or his soul, the free agent aims mainly at what his free will allows him, or rather commands him, to aim at, that is, right action, whose declensions are courage, justice, prudence, and temperance—in brief, action that takes on its form and color according to the catalogue of virtues. As I have already emphasized a number of times, action is at its core or at its summit commanding action, the command of action, the commandment of right action, and this command, far from injuring action, gives it its rule and its meaning.

It is true that reflective choice may consist in the removal of obstacles to the spontaneous deployment of our nature—including our nature in its necessary movement—in introducing institutions proper to modern freedom, in giving the force of law in certain circumstances to the maxim *laissez-faire, laissez-passer.* In a word, it is true that ancient prudence *can* consist in introducing or extending modern freedom. But in this case the agent will have concluded that the suppression of obstacles, the emancipation of certain tendencies of human nature was, in these circumstances and in this domain of economic or social life, favorable to the improvement of the practical capacities of members of society or of citizens, to their education for reflective choice. In such cases, the always difficult discernment of which belongs to the prudence of the agents and first of all of the legislator, the living-and-desiring-individual is not left to himself, abandoned to the freedom of necessity as if this were always and everywhere essentially advisable: thus untrammeled and liberated, he does not cease to obey the reflective choice of the civic body. In any case, in order to sum up the contrast between reflective choice and the freedom of necessity, a contrast that reveals the deepest stratum of the opposition between the liberty of the ancients and the liberty of the moderns, I would say something like the following: the free agent is concerned more with the intrinsic quality of his action than with the external obstacles to it, while the free individual is concerned more with the external obstacles to his action than with its intrinsic quality.

The Obstacle of Death

Since, in the perspective of modern freedom, life consists mainly in removing obstacles to life's movement, to its material and necessary movement, the free individual encounters death as the obstacle par excellence. This is in effect the singular posture of the living-individual engaged in modern freedom regarding death, not that he finds death undesirable or repugnant—this affect belongs to human beings as such—but that he considers it as an obstacle to avert, doubtless more imperatively than the others, but not at all differently. This obstacle is surely more intimidating, troubling, and fearful than other obstacles, but it belongs nonetheless to the same category of obstacles that modern life and freedom are determined to avert. Seen in this perspective, the death of the body does not open up a new domain, an unprecedented experience; it introduces no essential or urgent interrogation into the substance or the intimate texture of life. It is simply the greatest material obstacle with the potential of interrupting the material and necessary movement of life.

If the fear of death is thus the greatest fear of the acting-and-free-individual, since death is the greatest obstacle that opposes its movement, this fear takes on a very particular character: rather than surveying the horizon of life, rather than calling up thoughts worthy of its formidable magnitude, rather than inviting the imagination to evoke the splendors or the misfortunes that may await us beyond the tomb, this liberal and modern death comes to be mixed up and confused with all the material accidents that may be encountered in life, even the slightest, which now appear as bearing or indicating a risk of death. The security of the body, the preservation, comfort, and health of the body, become the most obsessive concern, even a more and more exclusive concern, of the living-and-free-individual.

A free agent does not relate to death in this way. To be sure, as I have said, and as is plain to see, he is a human being; he is naturally afraid of death and spontaneously seeks to avoid it. Yet it is not the standpoint from which he views his life: though he wishes to avoid death, he does not take it as his main task to avoid death; this is not the way he sees things. It is not that he is "more courageous," as the admirers of the "old virtues" imagine; even less is it the case that he is "mad" to the point of thoughtlessly risking his life as Nietzsche's "last man" believes and as we are led to think as individuals engaged in modern life and freedom. If the agent, the acting human being, despite his fear, his great fear of death, does not, unlike the free individual, spend every effort to avoid or avert death, this is precisely because he is an agent, an acting human being, and as such obeys his nature and the logic of action. What does this mean? Well, as we know, even if he is not the most virtuous of men, even if he often departs from the right way, as an agent he is in search of the right action, which has its rules and priorities and thus may include and even command acting in a way that implies mortal risk. It is not that he looks at death without blinking; it is that in acting he looks first at the rule of action, and death or the fear of death cannot be the main thing on his mind. One might say: the individual who sees in life a series of obstacles to avert ends up seeing in life only the threat of death, whereas the agent, finding in life a plurality of motives and rules of actions that it is important to combine rightly, sees before himself a very rich field of practice, which death, however much it may be feared, cannot come to occupy all by itself, nor even in general to dominate.

This orientation of modern freedom profoundly modifies the character of death. Now an external obstacle to avert or keep at a distance rather than an intrinsic factor in determining human life, a factor that must be given a place and a meaning, death tends to become an extrinsic accident that demands from us no effort other than the tireless and incessant effort required to make it more and more rare and to make it come later and later. This perspective is not incompatible, in certain circumstances, with anticipating a natural death that would have come later and bringing on a fatal accident, not in order to give death some meaning within life, but on the contrary to preserve its character as an extrinsic accident. In fact the modern state tends almost irresistibly to institutionalize euthanasia in one form or another. By taking the initiative to administer death before death imposes its own law, the state takes away death's power and its sting as much as it can; it withdraws its right to demand the attention and, as it were, the obedience of human beings. By administering death when it chooses and not at death's own time, the state follows to its end the mission confided to it by modern freedom, that is, to avert obstacles to the movement of life—which, in the last stage of life, leads it to want to prevent the suffering or dependency that hinder and, as it were, humiliate this movement: we suppose that putting an end to life deliberately preserves life's integrity more than letting it go to its natural end.

This very troubling intervention of the state is oriented by an idea of nature, or of life in conformity with nature, or of the nature of this life, and it is justified by this idea. This idea is nevertheless incapable of providing even a minimally rigorous rule or a criterion for the state's approach. To be sure, the intention is to preserve the continuity and the integrity of the feeling of immanent life, of the feeling of existence, in the most pleasant and least difficult and painful form possible. But how is this subjective feeling, which is so difficult to communicate as well as to penetrate, to be included in a practical approach? How can it be made the foundation of a public measure as serious as ending a human life? Neither the patient nor the intervening medical professional can derive a rule from subjective immanence with any confidence, first because such a rule would be essentially variable, like the subjective sentiment. Besides, and more fundamentally, since the point is to correspond to or to "match" a subjective feeling, it is impossible to conceive the approach that on this basis would put the medical professional in a position to judge and then to decide according to a passably objective and sharable criterion. There is no way to arrive at such a position on the basis of even the widest and most delicate subjective sympathy. Whatever a person's scruples and qualities, we are here outside the domain of a public rule or of law however these might be understood.

Thus the modern state, which has renounced the infliction of the death penalty for crimes determined by the law, tends more and more to grant authorization to administer death to sick people held to be at the end of life, according to a "law" that claims to determine what it is not possible to determine—that is, a certain "subjective state" of the person that would by itself justify and, as it were, require ending the life of this person. A "law" claiming to regulate the way the most universal and rigorous commandment—"Thou shalt not kill"—is infringed is the opposite of a law. However praiseworthy one may wish to consider the intentions of the legislator, we are forced to observe that the state now judges itself to have the right to authorize—that is, in practice, to encourage—the administration of death to innocent persons in a fundamentally arbitrary manner. This is the ultimate consequence, and by no means an accidental one, of the perspective of modern freedom, which defines death as an accident extrinsic to life.

The State and the Government

Let us return to the principle *laissez-faire, laissez-passer*, to the freedom of enterprise and the freedom of movement that define modern freedom, the freedom of the living-individual. This principle of freedom gives rise to or encourages the formation of a kind of active tissue, without command or obedience properly so called, that we now call civil society, a society peopled and animated by individuals who assert their rights and seek their interests. Civil society is *conditioned* by the state in the strong sense, by the state that commands no particular action but determines the conditions of all actions. As we have emphasized, as central and as decisive as the state is in shaping the life of modern societies, it neither governs nor commands in the proper sense. Moreover, beginning with the irruption of the democratic movement at the beginning of the nineteenth century, it has been thought, in diverse sectors of opinion, liberal as well as socialist, that modern societies could do without government as long as the state, by establishing and guaranteeing a framework of equality, allowed all members of society to produce among themselves an order that no longer depended on political commands, a *spontaneous* order. Curiously, these hopes were entertained under the banner of the minimal state or even the withering away of the state. This confuses the state and the government, an excusable and understandable confusion, given how difficult it is to discern the status of the modern state. Still, although the state and the government mix their efforts and often confuse their offices in the framing of modern societies, it is of the first importance to know how to distinguish them. Let us try.

Let us begin with an observation that is not often made even though it is plain to see. By establishing and guaranteeing the framework of equality, the modern state renders all government impossible in principle. Not only does it in effect delegitimize or eviscerate social commands, but it removes from all political government, all government in the proper sense, its condition of possibility. How can the state that is responsible for guaranteeing equality allow the deployment of the immense distance, the essential inequality, that separates one who governs from one who is governed in any political regime? In fact, I repeat, many believed that under the regime of modern freedom we would do without government. We know that this was a vain dream, a sterile speculation; modern societies or peoples demand and need to be governed as much as others. Yes, but how—since, once again, the state, by imposing the framework of equality, seems indeed to exclude the possibility as well as the legitimacy of a government? My riddle is quite innocent; I have no surprise waiting, since we all know the answer to the question of government under the conditions of the modern state; we all know how impossible government became possible: it became possible and legitimate by becoming *representative*.

Representative government is the great invention of modern politics. On the one hand, we owe to it the greatest successes of modern politics; or, rather, representative government has itself been the greatest success of modern politics. On the other hand, the equivocations of the notion have allowed or rather encouraged what is most perverse in specifically modern tyrannies. This is not the place to get into the question of the relations between democracy and totalitarianism.[2] I would just like to make a few remarks on the way the representative form of government affects and is affected by the question of action.

First remark: Applied to a political community, to a political body taken as a whole, the notion of representation is singularly confused, or at least very indeterminate. What is it that the government is supposed to represent; what does it in fact represent, and what in any case is the meaning of "representation" here? Is it to represent the members of the collective in their unanimity, or only a majority of them? Does it represent them according to their arithmetic sum or according to an internal articulation of the whole in its social, regional, or otherwise defined groups? Does it represent the interests or the opinions of these different groupings? And in each hypothesis what is the meaning of "represent"? We sense that these questions are infinite and that no response will be truly conclusive or entirely satisfying. This is because the notion of representation applied to a political whole invites us to consider all aspects of this political society from a perspective that is more theoretical than practical. We find ourselves before a problem of projective mathematics: given an indefinite set of sets to "represent," which should be chosen in order that the representation of the whole be as faithful or judicious as possible, and how are these sets to be projected in the most precise manner on the plane in which their representation will become visible? Practically all answers to such questions are to a degree plausible or defensible, since the questioning is not conducted under the constraint of a practical perspective or approach, but with all the latitude of a theoretical way of seeing, one that searches out the multiple aspects of a phenomenon. It is, moreover, this feature that has made the representative idea vulnerable to the ideological perversions I recalled above.

Second remark: While the idea of representation is dangerously theoretical, the idea that has guaranteed the prestige and the ascendency of the representative form of government and has attracted the favor of citizens in most of the countries of the world seems, on the contrary, eminently practical, that is, the idea of *consent*. This is an idea of enviable simplicity. It can be formulated thus: since no government is legitimate but one to which citizens have consented in advance by themselves or their representatives, only representative government is legitimate under the conditions of modern societies, in which citizens are too numerous to give opinions by themselves. Thus, the necessity of organizing consent provides the practical objectives that make it necessary to resolve the difficulties raised or left in place by the theoretical uncertainty of the notion of representation and to arrange things such that citizens recognize themselves in the consent thus produced—which means in practice that consent must result from *universal* suffrage, for any other method proves "indefensible" in practice. Still, we are not at the end of our troubles.

Third and last remark: The principle of consent provides, to be sure, a simple and radical solution to the problem of obedience. We owe obedience, we have an obligation to obey, only those who command or who govern to whom we have previously and explicitly consented. At the same time, this response leaves hanging the question of governing or commanding. One might as well say that it assumes the question has been resolved. It assumes that members of society or citizens will only obey a good government, or that a government obliged to obtain the consent of the governed will necessarily be good, or at least the best possible under the circumstances. This argument has a certain plausibility, but it does not get us very far, since it is perfectly circular. In any case, it neglects the qualitative dissymmetry that exists between commanding and obeying, the dissymmetry that I have emphasized with regard to action in general. The one who commands and the one who obeys have distinct points of view on each question; they relate to each by mobilizing different capacities and virtues. We think spontaneously that the governed, as "consumers" of government, are better judges than its "producers," but is this so clear? The principle of consent may take in all political legitimacy, but it tends to exclude from consideration, or rather to treat superficially, a major question of practical life, that of the virtues proper to one who governs or commands.

We can also clarify the oblivion of the practical question in the representative regime in the following way. Representative government presents itself as the government of society by itself. Those who govern willingly maintain this advantageous idea, and even if citizens have their doubts, they would much like things to be that way. If society governs itself by means of the device of representation, or if such a formula at least provides an approximately correct idea of what is happening, then the question of government is, as it were, magically resolved, or never even reaches awareness, since society cannot wish to be badly governed, and since the idea of government of the self by the self brings those who are governed and those who govern so close as to confuse them, such that the specific question of government cannot reach the light of day. The practical and political question (Who governs? How, according to what principles, and for what ends?) has been replaced by a theoretical and, as it were, optical framework in which government in a way reflects society and society recognizes itself in government, in a reciprocal transparency that can only be imaginary or ideological, so that the properly practical and political question cannot appear in its own form and greatness.

Now, once a statesman in a representative regime begins and commands an action on a certain scale, he modifies more or less significantly the society whose members consent to his government. Moreover, by modifying the constitution, or by establishing a new constitution, he has the means to modify the conditions of consent itself. In other words, as important as the "consensual" character of representative government may be, this character tells us little concerning the nature and the merits of governmental action. This action emanates from a starting point, some "high ground" that it consolidates and even exalts, or, alternatively, abases and degrades, according to its intrinsic quality, that is, independently of the popular consent, which, in a representative regime, is always in principle present. Consent does not create power or the site of power. Although power and the site of power surely vary according to the character of the regime, they are always already there, a given, since human beings cannot be without government. If a new government appears, it never springs up, as it were, from a simple absence of government, or from a state of nature; it follows upon or takes the place of a previous government. It follows, I repeat, contrary to what we like to believe, that governments are not, properly speaking, our own work or the product of our consent. We always intervene in an already governed world. The primary phenomenon in the human world lies neither in obedience nor in consent, but in the commands of those who govern. In truth, when we say that "we want to govern ourselves," we mean at the same time that "we want to be well governed, by a good government," that is, a government that has the intrinsic qualities of a good government, independently of the representative character conferred upon it by our consent. The device of representation has profoundly modified but has not abolished the *archic*[3] character of the political order, that is, of the human order.

Thus the living-individual who asserts his rights and pursues his interests, engaged in the *laissez-faire, laissez-passer* of modern freedom, is at the same time a citizen who wants to be well governed. As living-individual engaged in modern freedom, he willingly imagines, in various forms, a life without government. Since he must despite everything obey a government, he insists that this government "represent" him, a notion that can for him take on quite diverse meanings and modalities. Yet this is not sufficient. He still wants to be well governed, and he wants his country to be well governed. He wants the government's action above all to be just, or again perhaps prudent, or courageous, or even moderate—it must above all avoid too much debt!—the preference for one or another criterion bringing together citizens who share the same orientation, the same "sensibility," as we now say.

However considerable may be the innovations proper to modern politics, with, on the one hand, the state as guarantor of the equality of rights and, on the other, representative government—innovations that place the individual as citizen in a framework that is less practical than reflexive, a framework that obscures or even hides the question of action or of the intrinsic rule of action—political life, even under modern conditions, culminates and is actualized in the actions of those who govern. Although one who governs is always for us a "representative," "our" representative, this trait is, as it were, a recessive characteristic, for one who governs is essentially an agent, in action, whose being is wholly in the action that he is carrying out and who can only be judged appropriately and justly according to the criteria or rules of action. Since the natural law must be capable of guiding and judging action, its power to illuminate and its jurisdiction must extend to action par excellence, that is, political action. The natural law must be capable of grasping action not in the empirical regularities that action may present and that are of interest to less refined disciplines, but in the springs of its practice, in its motives and in its capacity to enhance and to improve the human operation. Natural law is not a rule foreign to human action, as would be a physical or metaphysical criterion elaborated by theoretical reason; it is a friend of action, *motivating* for action. It can judge the acting human being only because it knows how to guide and encourage him. We will consider natural law from this angle in our next and last chapter.

SIX

Natural Law and Human Motives

As we have seen in various ways in our previous chapters, the innovations distinctive of modern politics, whether they concern the idea of human rights or the establishment of the modern state and of representative government, have profoundly changed our condition by changing the conditions of human action. These innovations are particularly ambitious and audacious artifices that subject human agency to unprecedented constraints. Let me try to summarize this great transformation.

Since the human world is a world of action, a *practical* world, it is naturally or essentially *archic*.[1] Divided into commanding and obeying—a person either obeys or commands—it is also held together and put in motion by an act that begins and commands. Now, by a reversal that is indeed supremely audacious and ambitious, the initiators of the modern movement posited that there was nothing natural in this archic character; that, on the contrary, what was natural was the *an-archy* of a condition without either command or obedience; and that it was only by starting from such a condition that it would be possible to construct a just form of commanding and of obeying. Still, whatever the authority of our forefathers or of those who inspired our constitutions, it would nevertheless be hard seriously to maintain that equality is humanity's natural condition or that the command-obey polarity is artificial. As a matter of fact, the modern political order, *our* political order, has never ceased to be archic. Even today it continues to depend on the acts of those who command. If it were otherwise, we would not be so worried about the passions, reasons, and dispositions of President Donald Trump. Still—and here lies the transformation—the modern political project has introduced into the archic order what one might call certain an-archic planes—horizontal planes in a vertical order—which are ever more extensive and attract all public light to themselves and thus monopolize acceptable public reasons. Thus, even while we act and, as agents, as acting beings, enter necessarily into the countless modalities of the command-obey polarity, and necessarily engage in acts as commanded and illuminated by their rule, we seek to give more and more place to the plane of life that denies commanding or obeying by multiplying new rights, the declaration and recognition of which replaces the human life that we experience with a kind of "dream-life of the angels" in which we are supposed to put our faith. In chapters 3 and 4 I examined the weaknesses intrinsic in the very notion of human rights, emphasizing in particular how the increasing authority of this notion leads necessarily to a loss of the meaning and intelligibility of law. What concern me here are the consequences of these developments for our self-understanding. Under our present conditions, human association is more and more opaque to itself; it understands itself less and less, since, as the practical and archic operation is more and more obscured by an-archic conventions and frameworks, the bases of actions and of institutions and the sources of citizens' own actions and institutions are less and less accessible to them. How can we close the chasm, which grows larger every day, between our social and moral experience, on the one hand, and, on the other, the language of unlimited rights, which has become the sole authorized discourse? That is, how can we escape the demoralizing division between actual experience and legitimate speech and again give to our social and moral experience the means of expression that are so clearly lacking today?

In the face of an-archic individualism, with its rights that have no meaning except openness to an unlimited authorization of actions or behaviors with no rule or purpose, it is tempting to posit somewhat defensively a communitarian and archic order based on a natural law that derives its authority from a certain idea of nature, an idea understood as the objective synthesis of all norms desirable for the good regulation of the human world. This approach is a response to a very legitimate need, in the face of the virulence of the principle of subjectivity, to formulate anew the principles of an objective order. But this defensive and reactive approach, by advancing theoretical and synthetic propositions concerning human nature or the nature of the human world, remains a prisoner of the theoretical view that it shares with the philosophy of rights. It does not enter into the practical operation itself, which it claims to rule without taking the trouble to analyze how it works. In order to enter into the practical operation, we must first consider the question of human motives.

The Question of Human Motives

I will start from the following proposition, leaving it to readers to evaluate its validity and relevance as it concerns each of them: every action properly so called requires a balancing of the three main human motives, that is, the pleasant, the useful and the honest.[2] To this last we might add the just and the noble, which are kindred notions. There is no human being who is not moved by the pleasant, the useful, and the honest (the just, the noble). The active presence in us of these three great motives is not up to us, even though the strength of each, their relative weight, and the way in which they affect our actions vary according to our nature, our education, and, precisely, the way we are in the habit of acting. Since they are objective components of human nature, we have them in common as human beings, and it is because we share these motives that we understand each other and that we are capable of judging one another, and moreover that we cannot avoid judging one another.

One might argue that these three categories of motives are not equally natural or objective, or not so in the same way. The pleasant and the useful are notable for their stability and objectivity. According to a famous remark of Aristotle's, we cannot cause sexual intercourse to be unpleasant, nor a knife's cut to be pleasant. As for the useful, we cannot make it the case that forgetting to declare our tax liabilities would not be quite useful, or that others' failure to honor their debts to us would not be very disadvantageous. It is to the ideas of what is honest (just, noble) that we attribute a certain plasticity, to the point of refusing them a natural or objective status. It cannot be denied that these conceptions in fact vary considerably according to places and times. It is just these variations that have led to the elaboration of the human sciences—the sciences whose task it is to make intelligible the "infinite diversity of laws and customs" that humanity presents—and that the idea of an essentially constant "human nature" seems not to be able to account for. Nevertheless, as interesting as may be the epistemological or more generally philosophical questions posed by the scope of variations in the human phenomenon, these do not directly affect the practical human being, the human being in action, the agent. The question whether the idea of the just or the noble varies with one's particular culture is without pertinence for the acting human being: as an agent, he must count a determinate idea of the just or the noble—most often, in effect, the idea held and nourished by his "culture" or city—and not at all the "infinite diversity" catalogued by the anthropologist, as necessarily among the principal motives of his actions. The variability of ideas of the just or of the noble, but also to a lesser degree of the useful, and even of the pleasant (since human beings can have very different ideas concerning what is "good to eat")—this variability in no way changes the invariable fact that every human being, whatever the "culture" or city to which he belongs, is necessarily moved by these three categories of motives.

Of course this does not mean that the agent is the inert site of the activity of motives, of their play or of, as it were, the competition among them, or that the chosen action is determined mechanically by the strongest motive, or by the strongest combination of motives, however such strength might be evaluated. As I have just noted, the agent is an agent; he bears an active relation to his motives. Neither the pleasant nor the useful nor the noble (just, honest) is in his power, but the weight accorded to each and the way they are combined depend in the first instance on him, that is, on his disposition, on his nature as it is either perfected or degraded by his education and by the habits produced by his past actions. In brief, the agent's motives are not up to him, as to either their presence or their nature; they belong to the human being as such, to human nature; but the way these human motives become *his* action is up to him. His dispositions with respect to the action, his virtues and his vices, are up to him.

This description of the relationship between the action and the motives of action is admittedly just an overview, but it has the merit of emphasizing—rightly, I think—the objective and sharable character of human motives. But does it make sense to oppose the practical certainty of the agent as belonging to his "culture" or his city with the perplexity of the theoretical man confronting human diversity, as I have done? Let us take a closer look at the problem.

Let us start with the case, which is not so rare and which is always interesting, of a person who effectively or sincerely sacrifices the pleasant, or the useful, or both to his or her idea of what is just or noble. If we share his idea of the just or of the noble, or if we at least include it in the category of what is authentically just or noble, then all is well, I might say, and we admire such an agent. This is a just man, or a noble woman, and perhaps even a hero! But what happens when his or her idea of the just seems to us unjust, or when his idea of the noble seems ignoble? Can we still say that he has in practice obeyed, as an agent, the motive of the just or of the noble such as he understands it, adding only that for our part we disapprove, reject, or condemn his idea of the just or of the noble? Might we look at the crimes of Islamist terrorists who justify their acts by the commandments of their religion in this way? How can we reasonably confront the chasm that suddenly opens up between the point of view of the agent—occupied in this case by a terrorist—and that of the spectator—occupied in this case by a citizen informed of the terrorist's attack?

We cannot say that the terrorist's act is a crime that bears no relation to the idea of the noble or the just that he has taken from his religion or from a certain interpretation of his religion. Nor can we say that he has simply obeyed an idea that is inscribed in his religion or his "culture," an idea of the noble that we not only do not share but that horrifies us. Shall we say that he was led along and misled by a "false idea" of the noble? The truth is rather that his relation to the idea is gravely distorted. In such cases, we might imagine, the agent vividly experiences the passion awakened by a certain idea—a "sublime" idea—of the noble or of the just; he is carried away by this idea, but he lacks the adequate education or dispositions to lead his enthusiasm in the right direction and thus to purge it; he is looking, as it were, for a shortcut that promises to satisfy his passion immediately, in a way that is crude and cruel and that doubtless has little to do with the idea of the just or of the noble that originally motivated him or that was present more or less seriously at the beginning of the process. In the simplest case, which is not necessarily the rarest, this idea simply provided the pretext for satiating a criminal drive.

An analysis of this kind might help us to clarify the conduct of terrorists, but its merits are inseparable from its limitations. Its results are essentially negative; we avoid tempting errors without providing a satisfying positive explanation. The problem is not only that the "passage to the act" always retains something mysterious but also that we are dealing here with an aspect of the human soul that is especially opaque. It would not be wise to seek more clarity than belongs to the domain. The interesting inquiry concerns rather the general question of the place and the role of the "noble" in the architecture of the human soul—not only the soul of the terrorist or the jihadist but our soul, as peaceful citizens of our countries. The jihadist reactivates an archaic and crushing idea of the law in contact with a society that prides itself on having learned its lessons from the "war of the gods" and left behind it any commanding or demanding idea of the law.

The terrorist and the good citizens are opposed as the criminal and the honest person, but they share the same perplexity or incompetence, or parallel perplexities or forms of incompetence, where it is a matter of relating judiciously to the law. What other explanation is there for the fact that, when they attack our "pleasant" in the name of their "noble," we can answer them only with our pleasant in the place of our noble? In any case, it is futile to envision their conduct as the result of a "radicalization" to be treated by a "deradicalization," as if terrorist criminality were an illness separable from the general dynamic of human motives, motives *that we all share* and whose good ordering demands above all a *common education* that is sufficiently attentive precisely to the diversity of human motives.

Thus, the point of view of the observer and the point of view of the agent cannot be entirely separated. Once again, the observer, whether a professional scholar or an ordinary citizen, cannot say simply: this agent judges a conduct to be intrinsically noble or just that I judge to be intrinsically ignoble or unjust. However strange may be the "culture" of the "other," and however strange his idea of the noble or the just, I cannot judge an action without judging an agent, and I cannot judge the agent without judging myself. This requires effort. Thus Montesquieu, while emphasizing the "*bizarreries*" of the nobility's "point of honor," shows that the passion of the point of honor effectively sustains a vigorous disposition to liberty, since it introduces certain "necessary modifications in the obedience" due to a prince. Even if these "*bizarreries*" first strike us as incomprehensible and even seem to us absurd, the motive that informs them and that they in turn maintain then becomes quite comprehensible for us. The reference of human beings, whoever they may be, to an idea of the noble or of the just is always in principle comprehensible and sharable by all human beings, at least as a possible and meaningful perspective. If there are some forms of conduct toward which we cannot make this movement of understanding, whether these be "crimes of honor"[3] or of terrorism, then we must conclude that these are forms of conduct that are just as criminal for their agents as they would be if we had adopted them ourselves.

Moreover, as I have said, the acting human being is not a prisoner of his or her motives. He is not the plaything of his idea of the just. He is so much less its plaything as this idea is never completely determinate. Despite its sometimes crushing authority, it retains an irreducibly problematic character, or at least always presents certain "difficulties"—there is always something that doesn't quite add up. The agent moved by a high idea of the just, by a "thirst" for justice, may well come to correct and to rectify, or at least to inflect, the idea that he has received from his "culture" or his city. Thus those persons who are declared the most just have often been the "reformers" of their cities. In this sense the motive of the just or of the noble is "stronger" than the idea of the just or of the noble that specifies it here and now.

These remarks are intended only to suggest that the bases of practical life are much more stable and constant than we are inclined to admit, carried away as we are by the theoretical point of view of the social sciences, and more generally by the point of view of the observer or spectator. As spectators—and human beings *love* spectacles—we are naturally attracted and charmed by the spectacle of the diversity of human conduct that attracts our attention all the more when it is different from what is familiar to us, and that attracts it most especially if the particularity is spectacular, preferably spectacularly atrocious. This is not the best disposition for penetrating the springs of the acting animal. We must go against this tendency if we want to do justice to the point of view of action. All this matters for our approach to the question of natural law.

The Question of Natural Law

The very notion of natural law presupposes or implies that we have the ability to judge human conduct according to criteria that are clear, stable, and largely if not universally shared. It demands that the motley diversity of the human phenomenon, which is apparent to anyone, be reduced to a single set of characteristics common to all humanity and thus suitable to provide the foundation for rules of justice that are comprehensible and acceptable by all. I have suggested that the principal motives of human action—the pleasant, the useful, and the noble (just, honest)—constitute such characteristics. There is the question, however, how we can accord a decisive role to the motives of action—that is, to the factual bases of human acting—in an investigation into natural law, that is, into action's norm. How can we locate a valid rule of action on the basis of a description, however correct and precise it might be, of the way the motives of human action operate and fit together?

Sometimes we make a mountain out of a molehill. A case in point concerns the modern philosophers who are eager to reproach their predecessors or some of their colleagues for confusing "is" with "ought," or succumbing to the "naturalistic fallacy." But in reality there is neither a leap nor a chasm nor an abyss between "is" and "ought," but only a gentle slope along which we can walk with modest confidence. This, I say without vanity, is what I am now doing. To consider attentively the way in which human beings act, to grasp the reasons of their actions, and from this to discern the best way to judge and guide such actions—this not only involves no paralogism, it in fact constitutes the only way to proceed if we want to escape the alternative of deciding arbitrarily what rule, norm, or law we will declare valid or, on the other hand, renouncing its pursuit. This in any case is what I propose, and it is a modest proposition in all respects.

The principle of this proposition can be summed up roughly as follows: a society, a regime, or an institution that does not give sufficient place to the three great motives that we have enumerated, that does not open up sufficient space for them, cannot be considered in conformity with natural law, that is, with this order of practical life that is not made by human beings but within which they not only live better and more happily, in a way that is more in conformity with human nature and its vocation, but also find more complete and exact self-knowledge. I would like to show by a few examples that this proposition, though it may not provide for the elaboration of what the Greek philosophers called the "best regime," gives us the means to arrive at appropriate judgments on the great practical and political questions. As I have said, this is a modest proposition; strictly understood it leaves much to be desired and thus calls for complements and refinements. But it does help us arrive at practical truths on questions in which we collectively have a stake and that it is very important for us to evaluate judiciously.

Let us take first the case of a political regime concerning whose nature and merits much has been said over the last three quarters of a century, that is, the communist regime. Some are especially focused on communist "ideals," on the idea of justice that the regime claimed to put in practice, either in order to praise its radicality and completeness or to denounce its "utopian" character. Those who had granted the validity and the nobility of the ideal were then obliged to ask themselves whether this ideal was at least approximatively realized by the regime. There was thus an argument over about seventy years concerning ideal communism and "real socialism"—for how is it possible to judge whether the real corresponds to the ideal when one regards the real in the light of an idea of the ideal that is necessarily very uncertain, and when there is no way to know what a society effectively "in conformity with the ideal" of communism would really look like? Among the lessons to be learned from the terrible communist experience, let us retain this one: the surest way not to see what is right before one's eyes and to commit the most serious errors of political and moral judgment is to look at the human world according to the polarity between the real and the ideal, "is" and "ought." Once a person has subjected himself to the obligation to bring about the *convergence* of what he began by *separating* in the most rigorous manner, he is under a contradictory injunction that gravely prevents or falsifies any spontaneous or sincere perception of the human association under consideration, in this case, the communist regime. How can the sinister phenomenon—what we see as sinister and is sinister—be regarded as manifesting reality when it is supposed simultaneously to indicate the glorious ideal? How then can the sinister phenomenon even be *seen*? For that matter, how could one fail to see in the sinister phenomenon a manifestation of the realization of the glorious ideal that is all the more convincing in its paradoxical character? To be brief, called to see at once the real and the ideal, to see them as at once distinct and mixed up together, the observer loses the use of his senses and of his common sense.

Even so, it was a simple thing not to be duped, even without being seriously informed concerning the magnitude of the repression and cruelty of the regime. The most casual and least observant traveler, in seeing the sadness of housing and clothing, the stiffness and brutality of physiognomies, the difficulty of obtaining the most elementary services from one's neighbor—even the most naïve and favorably disposed traveler, I say, was forced to notice that the communist regime granted only the most meager share to the useful and the pleasant and that it frustrated cruelly and incomprehensibly these two fundamental springs of human life. This defect was so obvious and so massive that, whatever one's sympathies for the ideal proclaimed by the regime, and even if one were ignorant of the fact of its crimes, this defect was enough to declare it without hesitation to be contrary to natural law. A judgment based exclusively on the role of the useful and the pleasant in communist life would have been incomplete but also rigorously correct. This would have distinguished it from many other judgments, which were caught between the opposing tongs of the real and the ideal, the "is" and the "ought."

In order to establish the pertinence of the criteria of the three motives, we might also have taken the example not of a political regime but of a fundamental social institution such as marriage. If man and woman are to find in marriage a framework and a rule of life that gives appropriate place to the three motives, then a lot of imagination is not needed to unfold the practical consequences of a natural law so conceived. Marriage will not be an association of mere consent or enjoyment, one that might be chosen, put aside, and resumed according to changing feelings, as it is regarded more and more today; nor will it be a mere arrangement of the utility of families, as it was traditionally; nor, finally, will it be a paradoxical exercise in chastity, as proposed in a certain Catholic interpretation of the natural law that is still quite widespread. It may seem that the result of applying our criteria is, if not trivial, at least disappointing, since it leaves us with a concrete but minimal characterization of the institution, without providing any explicit criterion of perfection or at least of improvement. This objection seems to me groundless. The notion of natural law neither includes nor demands an exhaustive definition of all the institutions in which human beings seek human goods. It is supposed to help us apply a simple and concrete criterion for determining whether it is possible for human nature to find satisfactory fulfillment in a given institution, political regime, or framework of action in general. After this, nothing prevents us from pursuing the reflection on the engagement of each motive according to the institution under consideration, with the understanding that, in every human institution, but in different ways according to the nature of the institution, the motive of the noble or of the just opens up a field of possibilities to the desire for improvement that is incomparably more vast than does the motive of the pleasant or that of the useful. Natural law as I propose to view it here offers precisely this advantage: while providing explicit and concrete criteria that make it possible to appreciate the conformity of an institution or of a mode of conduct to the natural law, it leaves the agent as well as the evaluator great latitude for exploring paths of improvement, or rather encourages him to explore such paths of improvement. If we wish for the appeal to natural law to be able usefully to illuminate the complexities and refinements of practical life, it is important that, far from taking the form of a discourse that is theoretical and assertoric and that confuses the ordinary regime of action with the perfect regime, each one spoiling the other, the discourse of natural law maintain in a sense the potentiality and, I dare say, the reserve of practical principles that remain implicit insofar as they have not yet commanded a concrete action or institution, whose qualities can be assessed only after the action or the institution has been seen or experienced "in the act." The indication of modest principles of the kind I have just suggested fully leaves room for the motivating or even enthusiastic description of excellent practical realities, whereas the positing of a perfect law cannot usefully guide ordinary practical life or provide a sincerely desirable idea of practical excellence or perfection.

Such an approach would make it possible, along with other advantages, to avoid what is hazardous and occasionally ridiculous in *lists* of human rights. It makes little sense, we can agree, to include "paid vacations" in a catalogue of rights to be translated into all the languages of the world, including those that have no word for vacation or for salary. On the other hand, paid vacations make perfect sense among the both pleasant and useful measures that one might reasonably claim and establish in a productive society characterized by salaried work. It might be said that paid vacations, or other such policies, fit no better in an account of the content of the natural law than in a catalogue of human rights. This is true, but precisely, a right understanding of natural law, a right understanding of its *practical* character, saves us from the tyranny of the explicit and the exhaustive that is the fate and the scourge of the philosophy of human rights. This philosophy, having abandoned the perspective of the agent, can guide actions only by absolute propositions that can in no way enter into practical deliberation since, once a human right has been declared, there is nothing left to deliberate, but only strictly to apply. But the very character of natural law excludes anything so dogmatically explicit, since it involves the "play" proper to practical life, since it always leaves room to deliberate and then to choose. That effectively makes it less explicit, and moreover less pretentious, but not less rigorous: it alone is in fact rigorous *in practice* because, unlike declared rights, it is meant to be part of an actual deliberation and not to replace one.

So conceived, natural law is not like Kantian moral law, in relation to which the agent must always necessarily fall short. Natural law guides action but does not determine it, and thus does not command it. Only the agent, enlightened by the natural law and alert to particular circumstances, is fit to make the reflective choice that leads to effective action and commands it. Where the *natural* law is concerned, humanity in its ordinary or current condition is not this mass of perdition that the law condemns, but so many actors who undertake much and often fall short, who are ceaselessly straying further from and coming closer to this law of nature that does not define an ideal, but rather helps us to find the point of equilibrium and the optimal rule for a happy life, that is to say a reasonably pleasant, useful, and noble life.

I have already mentioned the common and, as it were, official objection that is addressed to the very notion of natural law: nature cannot make laws; only man, only human reason and will, are capable of producing law, since law has meaning only in relation to a human being who produces and obeys it. What is curious is that the force of this objection has been felt and even become axiomatic at the same time as and to the degree that we were losing any sense of the seriousness of human law, over a long process that I have tried to describe in these chapters. At the same time and to the degree that these human rights were gaining all the authority that had until then been accorded to political law—that is, the law that commands in the human world—the human law thus emptied of its meaning obtained the monopoly of the idea of law at the expense of natural law. This double movement suggests that natural law and human and political law, far from being incompatible notions, are on the contrary in solidarity and mutually implicated. Natural law is the law or the practical principles that human beings do not make because those principles belong to their nature, but that motivate, illuminate, and guide manmade laws. If there were not an authority or a resource like natural law, there could not be a human law in the proper sense, since human beings would not have a way to evaluate what they choose to call law, or, in the first place, no way to know whether what they are talking about is in fact the practical measure called law. Thus, as we see today, as the law becomes more and more exclusively a guarantor of rights, an authorizing law, it is losing entirely what constituted its nature as law, that is to say its character as a rule of action. It is true enough that the law followed by human beings has meaning only in relation to the human beings that produce it, but the natural law is precisely the mediator of this relation: human law has meaning only in relation to the *nature* of human beings. We might add that this natural law contains nothing that might offend human pride, since it simply invites the agent to combine the three great human motives in the best way. What could be more satisfying to the acting human being than to have produced, in the given circumstances, the action that imparts what is due to the pleasant, the useful, and the noble? What could be more honorable than to have discerned and produced the just proportion?

By ruining the architecture of practical life, the dogmatism of rights has destroyed the intelligibility not only of natural law and of human-political law but also of political command, of which political law is a part and which always provides the key to the practical order. However we might try to give new life and color to the now discredited notion of natural law, its destiny is inseparable from those of political law and political commandment. These three great constituents of the architecture of practical life either work together or perish together.

The Primacy of Command

If we close our ears for a moment to the ceaselessly whispered suggestion of *laissez-faire, laissez-passer*, if we strive to be attentive to practical life as we can observe it in ourselves and outside ourselves, then we will perceive that all action is either commanding or commanded, at least implicitly or by tendency. This, moreover, is why human life, whether public, social, or private is always essentially *in tension*. This is neither a defect that we should correct nor a disease that we should heal. There is no need to attribute this tension to some particular feature of human nature—for example, to attribute it, as Hobbes does, to the desire ever to acquire power after power or, as Locke does, to the continual uneasiness of a life besieged by need. Almost everything that presses upon or oppresses us is contained in the fact of having to act, in the fact of the *agendum*. It is in the urgency and the uncertainty of the *agendum* that the command finds and hides its root. It is in the tension inseparable from the *agendum* that even the agent least greedy for power finds himself led to command and finally obliged to command. The urgency of what is to be done and the desire to do well initially hide the command contained in the action itself; this command, which is at least implicit, of course does not escape those who take part in the action with us and who thus see a command, our command, where the agent sees only the thing to be done. Once finally deployed, the action has produced one who commands and one who obeys, each one possibly against his will, but rather in the end willingly, since such is the logic of action.

Thus command has less to do with the acting person's desire for power than with action itself; or let us say at least that the person covets the commanding stance only because it is internal to action itself. Authentic or complete action is naturally commanding. Command is action itself, its core and essence. As to one who neither commands nor obeys—who can say what he really does? In the movements of his body or of his soul, how can we discern the part played by habit, by reflexes, by automatic responses, by just going along, "doing nothing"? Command indicates immediately that one has broken with passivity, with the inertia of immanent life, that the present is not enough, that one cannot merely continue or prolong, that a future must be opened up and that an action *begins*. Aristotle emphasizes that only he who commands needs all the virtues of the acting person. (This is so at least of the person who means to command *well*, but then one who does not know how to command does not truly command.) He needs especially the virtue that orders and crowns practical life, the virtue of prudence, which is the virtue proper to him who commands, whereas he who obeys can be satisfied with what Aristotle calls right opinion, which tells him whom and how he should obey. In the good regime of the Greek city—that is, in the well-constituted democracy—every citizen commands and obeys in turn: either he commands, or he obeys—*tertium non datur* [there is no third option]. Among those who know what it means to command and to obey, no one would dream of claiming that he obeys himself or that he commands himself, a fetishistic formula and a paralogism dear to the adepts of "autonomy." These reflexive and reversible propositions have no meaning in practical life, since they presuppose that it is possible to erase the qualitative difference between the commanding agent and the commanded agent, between the disposition of one who commands and the disposition of one who is commanded—in brief they presuppose that the same agent can contain simultaneously the two opposing dispositions of practical life, as I have tried to explain in the preceding chapters. In the real city, which is inhabited and animated by actors and not reflective thinkers, the citizen can be said to accomplish no action that is not commanded by a magistrate of the city, unless he himself is a magistrate, in which case he commands other citizens for the time and within the scope of his office.

This perspective, which is oriented by the question of command, does not derive from some particular value attached to the superiority or inequality implied in commanding, or from some special taste for this inequality or superiority, nor from any overall conception of the world, from a "hierarchical conception" of the natural and human world, as is often said lazily and repeated confidently in dealing, for example, with Aristotle. This perspective is tied directly to a way of understanding practical life and action. The practical good, which has no existence outside of the action that aims at it and produces it, is, as it were, at every moment on the verge of being lost or degraded or of being abandoned. And at every moment it is the proper and personal aim of whoever has received or claims particular responsibility for this good and breaks with the inertia into which human life naturally sinks or gets bogged down to command and to begin the action that preserves or improves, the "perfecting" action, with a view to this good.

This practical primacy of commanding has been lost to view in the conditions of modern *society* and *freedom*, in which the irresistible power of the state and its sovereignty impose the framework and the habit of equal rights and thus offer a life that ignores command as well as obedience, at least ostensibly or apparently, a life that we call "free," a life in which everyone is busy day and night seeking the mirage of "autonomy." Command has not entirely disappeared—far from it; it is even seen as legitimate within the limited framework of a function within a system of productive work. It is in the guise of necessities of production or of administration that command and obedience subsist and are hidden among us. This, however, is by no means a residual subsistence, but rather a power that is all the more oppressive for being underhanded, given that "work relations" are all doubtless rendered more difficult by the fact that the inequality that there prevails is contrary to the principles of common existence and to the tenor of the rest of social life, where egalitarian familiarity rules. Let me observe in passing that, to the degree that the command-obey polarity became, as it were, invisible in the sociopolitical landscape informed by the figure of the autonomous subject, something called "domination" became the focus of attention; this was understood to be a social and moral phenomenon that is in a way detached from the action of members of society, since the command of the one who commands is no longer concretely inscribed and visible in the public space, but instead a phenomenon that bears down on the mass of society in a way that is all the more oppressive and discouraging. This domination has taken many forms throughout the development of modernity, but from the beginning it has been at the root of the resistance and suspicion to which modern productive society has constantly given rise. Certainly one of the most serious weaknesses of "liberalism"[4] is its incapacity to take the measure of this phenomenon, its readiness to see in this resistance and suspicion an "ideological" viewpoint fomented by those sectors of social or political opinion that refuse to see the "reality" or the "necessities" of "the modern economy."

It is, on the other hand, in close-knit communities that are devoted to action in the full sense, and where special attention is given to the correctness of action, to the effective presence and to the life of the good or of the proper end of these communities, that the articulation between command and obedience is the most explicitly clear and thematized, as well as carried out with the most care. This was the case in particular of the ancient republics, and it is still the case of Christian religious communities.

A s we have abandoned ourselves more and more completely, or more and more resolutely, to the inertia of *laissez-faire, laissez-passer*, we have lost sight of the central role of command in practical life, including especially the commanding role of the law as a rule of common action. We put our faith in the postulate that a certain inaction, or a certain abstention, is at the origin of the greatest goods.

At the same time as the flux that carries away human beings along with products of their activities swells and accelerates, we take off the brakes and abstain from actions that would tend to moderate and to direct the movement of people and of things. We believe, moreover, that nothing is more pointless or sterile in general than the tension proper to the acting person, whether he is concerned with this world or with the other. "Avoid stress," "stay cool," "take it easy"—these are a few versions of the only commandment whose validity we recognize. The grammar of human life has been reduced for us to enjoyment or suffering. Between these two modes of passivity that claim all our attention and provide the matter of all our new rights, there is no longer any space for acting. At the beginning of the arc of the development of modernity, we deliberately abandoned that law that commands and gives the rule to action, in favor of the state that organizes the conditions of action, an action henceforth judged not by its rule but by its effects. Since this beginning the rule of action has been continually eroded, and action itself has been continually shrinking, while the effects of our actions, amplified by our abstentions, have become ever more crushing. The acting animal is now the prisoner of the very audacious and ingenious arrangement that he once devised to escape the urgency and to avoid the difficulty of the practical question. Caught in the realm of inaction, he seeks out, in a kind of terminal fever, the last corners of social existence that still escape the *laissez-faire* idea and where the very idea of the law might suffer its final defeat. Western, or at least European, humanity seems to want to rally itself all together, not in order to do some great new thing but in order to refuse unanimously and irrevocably to hear the question: "What is to be done?"

And yet this passivity in which we place our pride cannot last indefinitely. The more the effects of *laissez-faire, laissez-passer* grow, the more urgent grows the question what is to be done.

APPENDIX

Recovering Law's Intelligence

Each era's agony receives its physiognomy from a certain tangle of problems, from a specific difficulty in responding to the primary human question: What is to be done? This difficulty is inseparably practical and theoretical; it concerns inseparably action and intelligence. Since human action is in the first instance corrective or rectifying, it presupposes as precise a diagnosis as possible of our situation as calling for a remedy, a diagnosis of our *predicament*—to take back an old French word that the English took from us, as is their habit. What then is our predicament?

I believe that the most precise way to designate what afflicts us, what troubles and demoralizes us, is to say simply: we no longer know what law is; we have lost the intelligence of law. The point is not to deplore that we disobey the law, that our morals are disordered, that the youth, as is often said, are without standards—all that is perhaps true, but the main point is that we no longer understand what the law is about. We no longer understand law according to its essence. We no longer understand law as the rule and measure of action. Our most urgent task is therefore to recover the intelligence of law as rule and measure of action. Thomas Aquinas is certainly the author who can best help us—Christians as well as non-Christians confronted with the loss of law's meaning—to carry out this task, if only we make the effort to understand his work in its full amplitude. The purpose of this presentation is nevertheless not so much to expound Thomas's restorative views as to examine our predicament more closely.

I have said that we have lost an understanding of law, or law's intelligence. We have not lost it by inadvertence or negligence. We have lost it because we wanted to lose it. More precisely, we have fled from law. We are still fleeing from it. We have been fleeing from law since we took up the project—let us call it "the modern project"—to organize common life, the human world, on a basis other than law. We have been fleeing from the law since we undertook to regulate our actions otherwise than by law, to seek the rule of our actions elsewhere than in law. This is not a matter of a moment's distraction or mistake. What is at stake is an immense enterprise to which we owe, for better and for worse, the driving and ordering of our common life over three or four centuries.

The adequate description of this enterprise cannot be my subject here. I shall limit myself to the indispensable points. If our actions are not to be regulated by law, then what shall regulate them? What kind of rule can replace law? We know that for a long time we have intended to regulate common life not according to God's or nature's law but according to human rights. Man is the being who possesses rights, and to live humanly is to assert one's rights. This new definition or determination is not sufficient. It still retains something negative or polemical: to assert one's rights is to "defend" them against those who deprive you of your rights, who harm or violate them, or against a society that is always curtailing them. In order to be able to order collective life completely or sufficiently, another, positive principle is needed, that of self-interest. The person who asserts his or her rights is also one who seeks his or her interests. Rights and self-interest are the two principles that allow for the ordering of the human world without recourse to law as the rule and measure of action. Of course we still have laws, indeed more laws than ever, but their raison d'être is no longer directly to regulate our actions but rather to guarantee our rights and equip us to seek our interests in a way that is useful or at least not harmful to the common interest. The sovereign, liberal, and representative state, by guaranteeing our rights, protects and encourages civil society, which is the framework within which we freely seek our interests. This is our political formula.

This immense political enterprise produces and presupposes a profound transformation of our humanity, as social beings and citizens. The person who asserts his rights and seeks his self-interest is no longer the agent for whom law provides the rule and measure of action. As the being who has rights and pursues his interests, he defines himself first of all in relation to himself, a relation that is subjective or subjectifying and by which he guarantees his independence with regard to any objective rule, that is, any law of God or of nature. This back and forth between self and self, this circle of self to self, verifies that the human being bears within his being no objective rule of action. In this sense the movement of subjectification according to rights and interests leads to the dismantling of the edifice of conscience or the preempting of its construction. The *habitus* that contains the principles of natural law must be deprived of force or validity in order to allow the subject fully to assert its right and its interest in the face of the right and interest of other subjects. The rule of action no longer resides within the agent but outside of subjects, at the interface where subjects meet each other. This strange exchange by which the subject deprives himself of the sure law that resided in his being, in his conscience, in order to go off in search of an indeterminate and unstable rule in the encounter with similarly disarmed subjects, this search for the self through the effacement of what gives the self its integrity, would merit a long examination, at once historical and systematic. Here we will limit ourselves to the consequences of this transformation of the agent into the subject.

These consequences range from the intimate to the immense: they affect what is most delicate for every human being as well as the whole of humanity in the way that it orders itself as a mass.

"The immense" refers to the world. Agents fleeing law have become subjects regulating their actions according to the world. Rejecting or leaving behind the laws of God or of nature—religious, moral, and political law that once regulated and measured their actions by making agents participants in a community, whether church, political body, or family—subjects have tended more and more to assert their rights and to pursue their interests in the unlimited space of the world by forming an immense system of action that has gained an authority over us that is without rival, under the name of the global market. The rule that the law no longer gives us, or that we no longer want to receive from the law, we seek very precisely at the end of the world, in these commandments that are sent back our way, with a power that subjugates the will and dumbfounds thought, by the world as the totality of human beings as rendered effective by the market or by markets. These are recent developments, but they were, as it were, contained in the Cartesian project of making us "like masters and possessors of nature." What is striking in this project is that it proposed an immense horizon of action, which opened up an unlimited career for this project, without attaching any rule or measure to it. Today the project has come up against its limit. We ask ourselves anxiously how to protect nature against its master and possessor; we seek in nature itself the law of our lawlessness. If what we have said up to this point has any pertinence, this question will remain vain. This is not to say that it is not necessary to preserve nature as much as possible, but the idea of protection in itself bears no rule of action any more than does the idea of the mastery of nature. We will effectively protect nature only if we rediscover the rule of human action, that is, law.

As I have said, the consequences of the transformation of the agent into the subject affect not only the immense but also the intimate. Since the subject flees law as such, there can be no rule for regulating the association in which the human being unites himself to another human being to found a unit capable of producing a new human being and thus continuing humanity. One of the most essential laws is that which, as it were, holds together the difference of the sexes with the difference of generations. The other sex is the strange proximity of that which is furthest away; the other generation is the strange distance of what is nearest. No human being can by himself regulate this distance or this proximity. To try to do so is to enter into a vertigo, a loss of the self from which there is no return. This is why laws of marriage and of filiation in a way make up the original laws of the human world. We have undertaken to abolish them in order to put in their place the freedom of invention and artifice of a subject defined in relation to his or her desire. In the place of the law that builds a bridge or sews a seam between the primary constituents of the human world, we put the project of a subject that means to remain in an infinite proximity with itself and thus to fabricate bonds at its pleasure. We often wonder today how homosexual activism was able to determine to such a degree the terms of the public debate, even though its legal claims are really and sincerely shared by a very small part of society. Homosexual desire places the relation to self in a position of inviolable sovereignty, since it cannot give place either to the natural difference of sexes or the natural difference of generations. By completely legalizing homosexual unions, we have achieved or intended to achieve a human world as detached from law as from nature, detached from natural law in the strongest and most pregnant sense of this expression. Homosexual desire, as desire, cares nothing for law. By nevertheless demanding to be legalized, it invalidates and abrogates law as such, law as the rule and measure of action. This is not true in the case of the law of heterosexual marriage, which is not primarily about heterosexual desire, but about the sexual difference. The legalization of homosexual marriage provides the modern project with something like its final destination, the proof that we have succeeded in organizing the human world without rule or measure, that we are finally living, and know that we are living, outside the law.

Thus, in the order of the immense as well as the order of the intimate, at the end of the mastery of nature as of flight from law, we are today equally without either rule or measure.

However violently we may be carried away by this conquest of nature and this flight from law, nevertheless each is reaching its limits. The limits to the flight from law are easiest to discern. We know with a certain knowledge that the difference between the sexes and that between generations, and more generally the need for a rule and measure of human action, will necessarily, if not gloriously, prevail against the excesses of the process of subjectification. One might even say that this process, by its very excess, gives plausibility to the notion of natural law, of a rule and measure of action that escape limitless subjectification. Doubtless such a law has never appeared as desirable as it does today.

Still, the desirability of such a law does not mean that it is *effectively* available. It is surely available insofar as Saint Thomas's elaboration responds fully and delicately to our need. At the same time, his "Treatise on Law"[1] has been available for centuries without preventing or slowing down our flight far from the law. Its authority has been marginalized along with that of the Catholic Church. To recover law's intelligence thus cannot consist only in carefully rereading Saint Thomas, as indispensable as this effort may be. We cannot proceed as if nothing had happened for seven or eight centuries. In order to make an adequate notion of natural law effectively available, we must measure the obstacles that stand in the way of understanding the long flight that has transformed agents into subjects.

Because we are carried along by the movement of subjectification, we tend to understand the natural as the moderns understand law, that is, as a limit on freedom—in the event, a desirable limit. There is no doubt that recent developments in our power over human life have sharpened this desire to set a significant limit on our freedom to exercise this power, a limit that is significant in the sense of giving meaning to the rule such that the rule can contribute to defining the fact of being human and to putting our humanity beyond our power. This perspective or this approach is surely legitimate and salutary. At the same time, it is purely defensive, serving only, in the best case, slightly to slow down an untrammeled power. This guardrail law, a law that posits limits to the technical interventions on life, thus calls for a complement, or rather a foundation, in the form of an encompassing law that, rather than fixing an external limit on limitless faculty of action, would propose instead to supply an intrinsic rule and measure of human actions across their whole spectrum. In brief, to go right to what seems to me to be the most important point, it is urgent to recover the fullness of law as practical reason motivating and regulating action, specifically action aiming at the common good. It is because he understands law in these terms and in this perspective that Thomas is so precious for us.

Having said this, we immediately take the measure of the difficulty before which we find ourselves. What we see as necessary quickly appears to us not only as difficult or very difficult but rather as impossible or, better said, as absurd. Why is this? Simply because it is against this practical reason as the motive and rule of action in view of the common good that modern political thought was built, and this by elaborating the arrangement based on rights and self-interest that we have evoked. It is true that the present difficulties and perplexities call upon us to reopen the case and raise the question whether the modern criticisms of practical reason as defended by Thomas, following Aristotle, were as well founded as the moderns have believed. Still, as preoccupied as we may be by the consequences or the effects of the modern project, we must admit that its original motives were not lacking in power. After all, this practical reason ordered toward the common good, so exquisitely described by Saint Thomas, did not make it possible effectively to order the common goods of the two cities, the earthly city and the church, or the city of God. There is nothing to add or to take away from the Thomistic analysis of the various kinds of law and their reciprocal relations, but it was not on the basis of this analysis that the order of European life was established. This order was established, on the contrary, on the basis of the radical critique carried out by another Thomas, this one the confessor of the modern state, Thomas Hobbes. In effect, how can this practical reason that motivates and regulates the search for the political common good as well as the religious common good—how can this practical reason discover the synthetic law of the human order when these two common goods are ordered by two distinctive legislative powers and two distinct laws? This mixing or confusion of two powers and of two laws, which led Christian subjects or citizens to "see double," according to Hobbes's amusing and illuminating expression, could not be unraveled and so had to be cut through. We are still living with the consequences—some of which are very positive—of this cutting, this energetic and intelligent decision, but a decision that simplified and even brutalized the order of the soul, an alteration or distortion that would only continue to worsen. However this may be, this decision consisted in depriving the church and, more generally, institutional religion of all commanding power and reserving this power to the political realm or to the state.

But this coup d'état—the expression is fitting—implied that commanding must find another motive or another basis than the law. It was in effect the notion of law as the rule and measure of action that justified the pretensions of the church and gave it an incontestable advantage of legitimacy over the state. But upon what may the commands of the political realm be established if not on the capacity to produce law that leads to the common good? You know the answer. The legitimacy of the state's commands will henceforth be based not on the promotion of the common good but on the protection of the rights of every subject. In order to cut through the knot of political and religious laws, people must be delivered from the law; they must be placed outside the law. It is starting from this position as outlaw, but an outlaw status that defines itself in terms of rights, that the human order will be recomposed, a recomposition that, as we said in the first part, is not only not finished but has lately taken on a strange virulence. The political order will henceforth presuppose and thus produce this lawless humanity that we know so well, this free and equal human being who founds himself on his self-relation. This is the political basis of the flight from the law whose power and duration I have evoked. Henceforth the human order—familial, social, moral, and religious—among us is suspended between a subject of rights that tend to the lawless and a sovereign political authority that claims to stand above all law.

This is not the place to examine how this violent artifice was made livable by the political genius and the moral resources of Europeans. Nor is this the place to consider, for example, the elaboration of representative government founded on the separation of powers. What yet must be noted in our discussion, though, is the binding and synthesizing power of Europe's proper political form, that is, of this nation that provided the framework in which the lofty sovereignty of the state and the ardent activities of subjects greedy for rights were reconciled between themselves and with familial, social, moral, and religious laws. This is the tightly and finely woven synthesis that today is in the process of unraveling.

I have not lost the thread of my discussion. It was necessary to recall certain points of history, even in such a hasty and compressed way, in order to bring out the motives that led to the abandonment of Thomistic natural law by those who might be called Europe's leading minds and to help us take the measure of the difficulty that must be faced in any return to this natural law. Would this not require deconstructing the whole political and moral history of Europe? At the same time, I have just mentioned, even more rapidly, the national synthesis thanks to which a nonnegligible part of the requisites of this natural law have been preserved and honored. What the present moment signals is the decay of this synthesis, given the unimpeded frenzy of the flight from law. The return to natural law thus takes on a different meaning than what it would have had or what it had in the eras of the construction of the modern project. There is no question of renouncing the separation of politics and religion, the necessity of which each of us can verify; the point is rather to recover an understanding of the law as such, such that the disordered extension of rights not be allowed to render unintelligible the very bases of European moral life. In an era when institutional Christianity has neither the capacity nor the desire to undertake the slightest project of domination, the invocation of "laïcité" or secularism, which has become ever more mechanical and insincere, serves only to block in advance any recovery of strength, however modest, on the part of Christianity as a religious institution. What once was an obstacle to the effective application of the Thomistic understanding of law—that is, the fact that it makes it impossible effectively to separate political from religious law—is no longer one, since what is in danger today is not the separation of political and religious law, but law as such.

To conclude, let me gather and extend the points already made. It is too late for us to limit ourselves to the defensive use of natural law that comes naturally to mind, as I have noted, when we aim to preserve a kind of minimal humanity against the assault of an unlimited artifice in the service of a disordered desire. To use a military metaphor, law's last line of defense is about to give way. We are required to be more ambitious. To recover an understanding of law in its plenitude is to recover the use of practical reason in the pursuit of the common good. This common good has a political component and a religious component, but we are no longer at risk of "seeing double." Hobbes's approach, which the secular party pursues obstinately, is now anachronistic. The problem is no longer to define the border and to order relations among two institutions, one political and the other religious, both equally ambitious and proud, but to measure the content in terms of the common good of this mixed law that has defined the Christian custom of Europe over the centuries and that is rediscovering an unexpected ordering power. The small number and often the timidity of those who propose or maintain it and the large number and often the aggressiveness of those who reject or despise it should no longer impress us. It is obvious to everyone that that part of public opinion that has dominated for so long and that intends now to finalize its triumph no longer has any idea of a government representative of a community of citizens. Along with a large part of the European political class, it has put itself in the service of an ideology of unlimited rights of the subject that has destroyed the very idea of a democratic government, or for that matter of a government that is responsible before the community it is charged with governing. The most sober way to recover this idea, by escaping from the paralyzing equivocations of the language of rights, is to hold together the idea of a human bond, of common action, and of a commanding law—that is, of practical reason in its commanding function. It is in the Thomistic analysis that these notions find their most illuminating articulation, provided that we read Saint Thomas in the perspective that belongs to him, which is also Aristotle's, that is, the perspective of a commanding and active political reason, and not only as a makeshift barricade for the party that long ago accepted its defeat.

Christians, and perhaps especially Catholics, are inclined, by a mixture of fear and disdain, to political passivity. In a country like ours, as I have suggested, they have moreover become accustomed to defeat. Saint Thomas teaches us to have more confidence in our practical reason and more esteem for our political task. When we act politically, we are not interfering with or usurping the role of providence.

We find in question 91 of the "Treatise on Law" in the *Summa Theologiae* a formula that merits our reflection on this subject: "Inter cetera . . . rationalis creatura excellentiori quodam modo divinae providentiae subjacet, inquantum et ipsa fit providentiae particeps, sibi ipsi et aliis providens." "Among all beings . . . the rational creature is subject to divine Providence in a more excellent way, in that it is itself made a participant in this Providence, by providing for itself and for others." Natural law, a part of eternal law, requires that we govern ourselves in the sense that we provide for ourselves according to our needs as rational creatures. This subject and this project, which every citizen who takes his personal as well as his civic life seriously and is well informed makes his own, can today be understood, formulated, and proposed in a coherent manner only within the Catholic Church, especially when this church is instructed by Saint Thomas. This is a political but a nonpartisan program, since the point is the reactivation of political responsibility as such, not the formation of some "Catholic party."

I propose these suggestions in a spirit of sobriety. I am not unaware that, when separated from the arguments that provide their basis, they must seem completely chimerical—whether one finds the chimeras pleasing or displeasing! Nor am I unaware of the doctrine with which all authoritative voices beat us down: we have left religion behind, and it can no longer be more than a private affair incapable of contributing to the orientation and even less to the government of the common world. I have also heard what is said of the de-Christianization of Europe, and I have observed certain of its effects. At the same time, I have observed the following: the forces that have pushed Christianity to the margins of European life and have for a long time threatened or promised to destroy it or replace it are now just as weak as it is. I do not mean only communism, now dispersed like Pharaoh's armies, nor socialism, which is nowhere to be found; I speak also of this imperious republic that a century ago inflicted upon the Catholic Church in France a political debasement that was humiliating but salutary. In this "immense plain and sleepy void"[2] that Europe has become, there remains but one spiritual force still ascendant, the one to which I have devoted a good part of this discussion and which demands with virulence that subjective rights be absolutized.

Even so, I affirm with tranquility, its weakness and sterility are inscribed within its very project. It can only and wishes only to undo and to unbind; it does nothing but render us every day more immobile in our languor and impotence, by turning us away from a common good capable of caring for and governing itself. The kind of panicked perplexity that has gripped Europeans and continues to spread, whatever may be the vicissitudes of the Euro, is the helpless disarray of an immense population of rich talents and resources but whose fate is no longer the responsibility of any true government. The regulatory regime under which we have labored for twenty years signifies the disappearance of all political prudence in Europe. Europeans see their continent, once master of the world, slide toward political insignificance but are not moved. Either this decline will proceed to an inglorious end, or the need finally to govern ourselves again will meet the proposition of high political prudence contained in the Thomistic natural law teaching. In this case, the need and the proposition drawing life from each other, we will open the way not to a renewed European domination (which is neither possible nor desirable) but, through the common action of European nations, to a reestablishment and renewal of the physiognomy of our continent, a recovery of a political and spiritual history that is now about to end. The renewed confidence in our common destinies will help us to look up once again toward divine providence. Europe's religious destiny is not written in the statistics of baptisms or confirmations; it depends on the common action of European nations, an action that we will either know how to carry out, according to the inseparably civic and Christian perspective that is the very meaning of Europe, or we will not. This destiny is thus as precarious as all human things, that is, as dependent equally on our wisdom and on our prayers.

NOTES

Translator's Introduction

1. Pierre Manent, *Seeing Things Politically*, trans. Ralph C. Hancock (South Bend, IN: St. Augustine's Press, 2015).

2. Manent, *Seeing Things Politically*, 203.

3. Spinoza: a being's sheer perseverance in being. See *Ethics*, part 3, beginning. Hobbes, throughout his *Leviathan*, and beginning in the very first chapter, translates *conatus* as "endeavour."

4. Daniel Mahoney (above, in the foreword) captures Manent's understanding perfectly in the traditional phrase "liberty under law."

5. Thomas Aquinas, *Summa Theologiae* II-II, q. 91, quoted by Manent in the appendix, "Recovering Law's Intelligence."

ONE   Why Natural Law Matters

1. The six chapters of this book are based on six lectures delivered in March 2017 at the Institut Catholique de Paris. The Étienne Gilson Chair was founded in 1995 on the occasion of the centennial of the institute's Faculté de philosophie. Named in honor of the twentieth century's greatest historian of medieval ideas, the institute wishes to be the means of a new inquiry concerning metaphysics, its history, and its contemporary standing

in the diverse philosophical traditions. Since its creation, it has each year invited one person known for his contribution to historical or speculative research in the metaphysical domain to deliver a series of six lectures in French.

2. Olivier Roy, *Le Djihad et la Mort* (Paris: Seuil, 2016), 99, 161.

3. Rousseau, *On the Social Contract*, bk. 1, ch. 6, in *Oeuvres complètes* (Paris: Gallimard, 1964), 3:360 [trans. Hancock].

TWO   Counsels of Fear

1. In the language of modern "contractualist" political philosophy, this reduction takes the form of the proposition according to which society is not natural to humanity, or that humanity is not naturally sociable. This proposition must be understood in a dynamic sense: the power and the right of nature for humanity do not reside in association but in separation.

2. See for example Thomas Hobbes: "These small beginnings of Motion, within the body of Man, before they appear in walking, speaking, striking, and other visible actions, are commonly called ENDEAVOUR. This endeavour, when it is towards something which causes it, is called APPETITE, or DESIRE . . . and when the Endeavour is fromward something, it is generally called AVERSION." *Leviathan*, ed. C. B. Mcpherson (Harmondsworth: Penguin, 1968), ch. 6, p. 119. It is of course in Spinoza that the notion of *conatus* takes on the most marked "metaphysical" character. See in particular propositions 6–9 of bk. 3 of the *Ethics*.

3. Translator's note: see ch. 3, n. 8, on the extensive connotations of Manent's term "operation."

4. See Hobbes, *Leviathan*, ch. 11, p. 161.

5. See introduction to Hobbes, *Leviathan*.

6. Niccolò Machiavelli, *The Prince*, trans. Harvey C. Mansfield Jr. (Chicago: University of Chicago Press, 1985), p. 61.

7. "I gently take human beings as they are," says Philinte the "realist." Moliere, *The Misanthrope*, 1.1 [trans. Hancock].

8. As Alceste the "idealist" says (ibid., 5.4).

9. Translator's note: Head or chief of a company of mercenaries (Italian).

10. "So Giovampagolo, who did not mind being incestuous and a public parricide, did not know how—or, to say better, did not dare, when he had just the opportunity for it—to engage in an enterprise in which

everyone would have admired his spirit and that would have left an eternal memory of himself as being the first who had demonstrated to the prelates how little is to be esteemed whoever lives and reigns as they do; and he would have done a thing whose greatness would have surpassed all infamy, every danger, that could have proceeded from it." Machiavelli, *Discourses on the First Ten Books of Titus-Livy*, trans. Harvey C. Mansfield and Nathan Tarcov (Chicago: University of Chicago Press, 1996), bk. 1, ch. 27, p. 63.

11. Machiavelli, *Prince*, ch. 17, p. 67.

12. Machiavelli, *Discourses*, bk. 1, ch. 47, p. 98; bk. 3, ch. 6, p. 229; ch. 21, p. 263.

13. Machiavelli, *Prince*, ch. 18, p. 70.

14. Ibid., ch. 7, at the end.

15. "What is the use of these lofty points of philosophy on which no human being can settle, and these rules that exceed our use and our strength? I often see people propose to us patterns of life which neither the proposer nor his hearers have any hope of following, or, what is more, any desire to follow. . . . It would be desirable that there should be more proportion between the command and the obedience; and a goal that we cannot reach seems unjust." Montaigne, *The Complete Essays*, trans. D. M. Frame (Stanford, CA: Stanford University Press, 1958), 756, 757 (bk. 3, ch. 9).

16. *Prince*, ch. 18, p. 70.

17. Ibid., ch. 26.

18. Machiavelli, *Discourses*, bk. 1, preface, p. 6.

19. Ibid., bk. 3, ch. 1, p. 212.

20. Machiavelli, *Prince*, ch. 15, p. 61; ch. 18, p. 70.

21. Emerging in the context of Christianity, the notion of conscience supports and complements the Aristotelian analysis of practical life and of reflective choice so well that the two elements prove to be inseparable; once the notion of conscience is dismissed, modern practical philosophy (if these two adjectives can indeed be put together) will no longer be able to find its way in practical reasoning.

22. Luther, *The Bondage of the Will*, in *Luther and Erasmus: Free Will and Salvation*, ed. E. Gordon Rupp and Philip S. Watson, Library of Christian Classics 17 (Philadelphia: Westminster, 1969), 261–62.

23. Ibid., 190.

24. Ibid., 305–6.

25. Thomas Aquinas, *Summa Theologiae* II-II, qq. 2 and 4.

26. As Thomas emphasizes in the article *Utrum homo possit scire se habere gratiam*, since God, the principle and object of grace, is unknown to us

owing to his transcendence, his presence or absence in us cannot be known to us with certainty. Ibid., I-II, q. 112, a. 5.

27. Luther, *Bondage of the Will*, 309.

28. "Hoc est *artis*, transilire a meo peccato ad justitiam christi, das ich so gewiss weis, das Christi frumkeitt mein sei, so gewiss ich weis, dass dieser Leib mein sei." *Table Talk*, cited in J. Maritain, *Trois réformateurs* (Paris: Plon, 1925), 25. One might perhaps translate as follows: "It is quite an *art* to leap from my sin to the justice of Christ, and thus to be as certain that Christ's piety is mine as I am certain that this body belongs to me."

29. Luther, *Bondage of the Will*, 109–12.

30. Ibid., 200–201, 206–7.

31. Ibid., 127.

32. This point is perfectly developed by John Calvin in *Institutes of the Christian Religion*, 3.19, "Christian Freedom." See, e.g., John Calvin, *Institutes of the Christian Religion*, ed. John T. McNeill, trans. Ford Lewis Battles, Library of Christian Classics 20–21 (Philadelphia: Westminster, 1960), 833–49.

T H R E E   The Order of the State without Right or Law

1. Hobbes, *Leviathan*, ch. 15, p. 217; also ch. 26, p. 314.

2. Ibid., ch. 15, p. 211.

3. Except, in a sense, for the law that enjoins us to seek peace, which, as we have seen, is not properly a law. (See n. 1 above.) There is no law that determines the justice or injustice of human actions but the law of the sovereign: "And the Makers of Civill Laws, are not only the declarers, but the Makers of the justice, and injustice of actions, there being nothing in mens Manners that makes them righteous, or unrighteous, but their conformity with the Law of the Soveraign." Hobbes, *Leviathan*, ch. 42, p. 586.

4. Ibid., ch. 14, p. 190.

5. One can say that it has no meaning because, and as long as, it has no effectiveness, but this is to confirm that, in the state of nature, it has no meaning.

6. The changes in laws and in behaviors produced by the civil rights movement in the United States provide what is doubtless the most eloquent and convincing example of an extension of rights that enlarges and deepens the meaning of the human association itself.

7. Rousseau, "Lettre à Christophe de Beaumont," in *Œuvres complètes*, Bibliothèque de la Pléiade (Paris: Gallimard, 1969), 4:936. "He is an animal" confirms and intensifies "he is nothing," meaning that the being in question has no human characteristics.

8. Translator's note: *Opération* is a rich term in P. Manent's French, resonating with the Latin "operatio," which, in Thomas Aquinas's thought, and then in Dante's usage in *De monarchia*, for example, indicates the active realization of a naturally ordered function, an activity that is by nature meaningful because it participates in the synthesizing production of a whole that is good. Of course the term does not carry its full, premodern implications when the author applies it to modern authors and processes. I render it typically by the admittedly paler English equivalent "operation."

9. Machiavelli, *Prince*, ch. 9, p. 39.

10. Hobbes, *Behemoth*, ed. F. Tönnies (London: Frank Cass & Co., 1969), dialogue 4, p. 159.

11. Leo Strauss, *The Political Philosophy of Hobbes: Its Basis and Its Genesis* (Chicago: University of Chicago Press, 1952; first published in 1936), 149–52.

FOUR   The Law, Slave to Rights

1. See footnote on the Greek term *archē* (ἀρχή) at the beginning of ch. 6.

2. Only a political body can give itself a law and thus be "autonomous" or "independent." As Thomas Aquinas sums up the matter, one can only say "each is himself the law . . . insofar as he takes part in a [collective] order regulated by some government." *Summa Theologiae* I-II, q. 90, a. 3. To use the terms rigorously, no one can give a law to his own actions: *nullus, proprie loquendo, suis actibus legem imponit.* I-II, q. 93, a. 5.

3. It must be noted that today's campaigns that aim at discouraging smoking emphasize self-mastery much less than health. In the world of autonomy, self-mastery cannot be a significant objective or moving force.

4. Montesquieu expresses himself prudently but inopportunely on this point: "The idea of empire and of domination is so composite, and it depends on so many other ideas, that it is not one that he [man] would have at first" (*The Spirit of the Laws*, 1.2 [trans. Hancock]). If he does not have it at first, he will never have it. Montesquieu can envision a development of

growing complexity since he makes use of the impressive but vague notions "empire" and "domination." The notion of command has a simplicity and density that make it impossible to see it as the result of a composition of primitive ideas empty of any "note" of command.

5. Translator's note: A reference to the elegant manners of a woman in Baudelaire's poem "À une passante" (To a woman passing by).

6. Translator's note: These Greek terms denote mastery or lordship, the masculine and feminine forms perhaps suggesting civil and ecclesiastic government.

FIVE   The Individual and the Agent

1. This is the complete form of the phrase (roughly: "Let it be, let it go")—more commonly known by just its first half—first proclaimed in the eighteenth century in the cause of economic freedom. It is attributed to the French economist Vincent de Gournay.

2. Totalitarianism—that is, specifically modern tyranny—is based on an ideological version of representation: the "party," in the name of the "class" or the "race," claims to represent the "people," or at least the "better part" of the people. Hence the perverse mechanism of a succession of identifications, which is particularly explicit in the case of communism and has often been noted: the secretary general "represents" the party, who "represents" the proletariat, who "represents" humanity in the final stage of its emancipation.

3. On the meaning of "archic," see the first note in ch. 6.

SIX   Natural Law and Human Motives

1. Translator's note: Manent here is drawing upon the Greek term *archē* (ἀρχή), which associates a beginning with an act and therefore with ruling. Compare the connotations of our term "principle"—a ruling origin.

2. Translator's note: The French *honnête*, rendered here "honest," is a more capacious term than our English "honest" has become, as the author suggests in the following sentences. It carries connotations including what is fair, decent, upright, and honorable.

3. Translator's note: The author alludes to the killing of a girl whose father or brother considers her to have misbehaved.

4. Translator's note: "Liberalism" is here used in the European sense, which refers not to the left of the political spectrum but to the political doctrine that favors capitalism and the free market as well as, more generally, the idea of individual rights.

APPENDIX   Recovering Law's Intelligence

1. See Thomas Aquinas, *Summa Theologiae* I-II, qq. 90–108.

2. "Et dans la plaine immense et le vide dormeur . . ." From the poem "Le moulin," by Émile Verhaeren.

INDEX

action, 83–99
  Christianity and, x, 35, 37, 39–40
  commands and, xvii, 53, 113–17
  common good and, vii
  as corrective, 119
  death and, 89–92
  explicit and implicit and, 111–13
  human rights and, 117, 120–21, 128
  laissez-faire, laissez-passez, and,
    86–89
  law and, 119–21
  liberty under law and, ix, xvii
  modern political philosophy and, xii,
    24, 25, 75, 83–84, 92–98, 99,
    113–17
  motives, human, and, xv, 103
  natural law and, viii, 98, 121–22
  obeying and, 53
  order and, ix
  practical question and, 60–62
  practical reason and, viii, xv, xvii
  predicament of, 119–20
  Providence and, xvii, 128–30
  prudence and, xvii
  as theoretical and practical, 23, 119
  virtues and, vii
Ancients and Moderns, quarrel of, 25
Aquinas. *See* Thomas Aquinas
archic character of action
  commands and, xxiii, 99–100
  conscience and, xi–xii
  grounding nature of, xii
  human motives and, xv
  human nature and, 100
  human rights and, 100–101
  liberty under law and, xii
  modern political philosophy and,
    97, 99–100
  natural law and, xii
  obeying and, 99–100
  overview of, ix, 99
  practical reason and, xi–xii, xv,
    xxiii
  twin pillars of, xi–xii
Aristotle
  Christianity and, 55
  commands and, 114
  conscience and, xi

Aristotle (*cont.*)
deliberation and, xxi
friendship types and, xxiv
human motives and, 102
human nature and, 50
means and ends in, xxi
modern political philosophy and, 20, 24
practical reason and, xv, xxi, 125, 128
prudence and, x–xi, xiv
Socratic political science and, 54
Aron, Raymond, xvi
autonomy
commands and, 114–15, 116
as *conatus*, xxiii
criticism of, viii
domination and, 116
as groundless, viii
heteronomy and, 66
human nature and, 65
human rights and, xxiii
law and, 65–68, 135n2
legitimacy and, xiii
marriage and, xvi
modern political philosophy and, xiii, 65–67
practical reason and, viii, xxiii
self-mastery and, 67, 135n3

barbarity, 6, 78
Bayle, Pierre, xiii, 87
Beyond Radical Secularism (Manent), vii

Capelle, Philippe, 1
Catholic Church, xiii, 56, 58, 75, 124, 129
Christianity and Christians
action and, x, 35, 37, 39–40
Christian Question and, xxii, 54–57
city of God and, xxi
classical philosophy and, xxi

common good and, 128
communism and, 129
conscience and, x–xi, xxi, 36, 40–41, 133n21
death and, xiv
de-Christianization of Europe, 129–30
Europe and, xxv, 54–57, 129–30
faith and, 37, 38
freedom and, 87–88
free will and, x, 40, 87–88
God and, 40
grace and, 37, 55
human nature and, 34–41
human rights and, 8
interiority and, 56
Islam and, ix
LGBT rights and, ix, 5
liberalism and, 88
liberty under law and, viii, xi
modern political philosophy and, xxi, xxii, 54–57, 84, 87
natural law and, xi, 8–9, 124, 127
practical reason and, xiv, xxi, 35, 125
Protestant Reformation and, 37, 40
sin and, 55
social knowledge and, 56–57
tolerance and, ix
city of God, xxi, 125
civil rights movement (US), 134n6
commands
action and, xvii, 53, 114, 117
archic character of, xxiii, 99–100
autonomy and, 114–15, 116
command-obey and, 65, 70–71, 100, 116
equality and, 115–16
freedom and, 88, 115
human nature and, xii, xix, 113, 114, 115
human rights and, 128

law and, 125–26
modern political philosophy and, xii,
   60–71, 113, 115, 116
natural law and, 113–14
obeying and, 114, 115
passivity and, 114, 117–18
practical primacy of, 113–17
practical reason and, xii, xvii, xxiii,
   xxvi
virtues and, xxiii, 95–96, 114
common good, vii, xiii, xxi, xxv,
   124–26, 128, 130
common sense, xx, 13, 14, 17, 66,
   109
communism
   Christianity and, 129
   human nature and, xvi
   ideals of, 108–9
   marriage and, 109–10
   motivation and, 109
   naturalistic fallacy and, 108
   natural law and, xvi, 108–9
   preoccupation with ideals of, xvi
   shortcomings of, xvi
   socialism and, 108
   totalitarianism and, xvi
conatus, xiii, 20–22, 50, 53, 81, 86,
   131n3, 132n2
conscience
   archic character of, xi–xii
   Christianity and, x–xi, xxi, 36,
      40–41, 133n21
   erasure of, 36
   free will and, xi, 39
   human nature and, 36
   knowledge of, xi
   liberalism and, xiii
   modern political philosophy and,
      133n21
   natural law and, x–xi
   overview of, x
   as perspective of God, x

practical reason and, x–xi
   substantive conception of, x
courage, vii–viii, xiv, xv, 44, 88
cultural relativism, ix

death
   Christianity and, xiv
   death penalty and, xiv, 92
   euthanasia and, xiv
   as extrinsic accident and, xiv
   freedom and, 89–92
   human dignity and, xiv
   liberty under law and, xiv
   modern political philosophy and,
      xiv, 89–92
   practical reason and, xiv, xxiv
   as *summum malum*, xiv
Declaration of the Rights of Man and
   of the Citizen (1789), 47
deconstruction, xxiii, 10, 13, 53, 73, 127
Descartes, René
   "like masters and possessors of
      nature," 122
Discourses, The (Machiavelli), 35
Durkheim, Émile, 73

equality
   commands and, 115–16
   human nature and, 11
   human rights and, xx, 4–5
   modern political philosophy and,
      84–85, 93
   natural law and, 4, 11–12
Europe
   action and, 130
   Christianity and, xxv, 54–57,
      129–30
   church and state in, xx
   future of, 130
   human rights and, xiii
   natural law and, 127
euthanasia, xiv, 91

fact-value distinction, x, xv, xx–xxiii, 107
faith, xxi, 37–41, 55–56, 100, 116
fear, xxii, 30–31, 33–34, 43, 44–46
freedom
    Christianity and, 87–88
    civil society and, 92
    commands and, 88, 115
    consciousness and, 85
    death and, 89–92
    homosexuality and, 86
    human nature and, 5–6, 9, 23–24
    human rights and, 5–7, 12–13
    laissez-faire, laissez-passer, and, 86–89, 92, 97, 113, 116, 117, 136n1 (chap. 5)
    law and, 123
    modern and classical conceptions of, 85–89
    modern political philosophy and, 69–75, 85–89, 91–93
    natural law and, 7–8, 85–86
    as nature unbound, 86–87
    reflective choice and, 86–88
    sexual freedom, 86
    virtues and, 88, 90
free will
    Christianity and, x, 40, 87–88
    conscience and, xi, 39
    liberalism and, xiii
    modern political philosophy and, x, 87–88
    natural law and, viii, xii
    practical reason and, x, xii, xviii
    Reformation and, 39

Giovampagolo of Perugia, 32, 132n10
gnoseological situation, 28, 30, 37
God, city of, xxi, 125
good, the
    divine goodness and, xxiv
    primacy of, xviii

    secularism and, vii
    support for, vii
Gournay, Vincent de, 136n1 (chap. 5)

heteronomy, viii, 66
Hobbes, Thomas
    city and, 52
    conatus and, 132n2 (chap. 2)
    death and, xvii
    fear and, 44–46
    freedom and, 87
    human motives and, 21–22
    human nature and, 112–13
    moralizing fear of, xxii, 44–46
    natural law and, xii, xvi, 44, 128
    obeying and, 60, 64, 67–68
    practical reason and, 125
    sovereignty and, 58–59, 60
    state of nature and, viii, xiv, 21–23, 46
homosexuality
    freedom and, 86
    human nature and, xx, 14
    human rights and, xx, 16–17, 79
    law and, 79–80, 123
    marriage and, ix, 16–17, 123
    as metaphysical demand, xx
    naturalization of, 14–16
    natural law and, xx, 14, 16–17, 123
    sex and, 14–17
    tolerance and, 17
human nature
    archic dimension of, 100
    autonomy and, 65
    biology and, 9–11
    Christianity and, 34–41
    commands and, xii, xix, 113, 114, 115
    communism and, xvi, 108–9
    conscience and, 36
    culture and, 9–11
    deconstruction and, 11–13
    denaturalization and, 9–14
    equality and, 11

discrediting of, 1–2, 34

displacement by human rights of, viii

equality and, 4, 11–12

eternal law and, xvii

fear and, 30–31

as free action, xxiv

freedom and, 7–8, 85–86

free will and, viii, xii

globalization and, 3–4, 7

ground of, xxiv

homosexuality and, xx, 14, 16–17, 123

human diversity and, xv

human nature and, 6–10, 110, 112

human rights and, xvii, 1–2, 6–9, 111, 113

imagination and, 29–30

importance of, 1

institutions and, 110

judgment and, 12

liberty under law and, ix

marriage and, ix, xvi, 16–18, 109–10

modern political philosophy and, xii, 55, 62, 98, 127, 132n1

motivation and, xxiv, 101–4, 107–8, 111–13

naturalistic fallacy and, 107

naturalness of, 9–12, 111–12

obeying and, 7, 28

positive law and, 112

practical reason and, xxiv, 111, 124–25, 129

question of, 106–10

realism and, 28

recovery of, xxv

renewed interest in, 1–2

return to, 127

state of nature and, 7–16

subjectification and, 124

terrorism and, xv–xvi

universality of, 106–7

nature. *See* state of nature

Nicomachean Ethics (Aristotle), xi

obeying

  action and, 53

  archic aspect of practical reason and, 99–100

  command-obey and, 65, 70–71, 100, 116

  commands and, 114, 115

  consent and, 95–96

  modern political philosophy and, xii, 21, 23, 31, 58–62, 63–71, 95

  motivation and, 21, 37

  natural law and, 7, 28

  sovereignty and, 64

  virtues and, 95–96

On Free Will (Erasmus), 37

order, ix, 51, 58, 70–73, 93, 97, 126

passivity, 78, 81, 114, 117–18

Paul (saint), xi, xiv

philosophy. *See* modern political philosophy

Plato, xiv, xv, 24

the pleasant, useful, and honest, xi, xv, xxiv, 101–6, 107, 109–13. *See also* motives, human

political action. *See* action

practical reason

  action and, viii, xv, xvii

  archic character and, xi–xii, xv, xxiii

  authority and, xiv

  autonomy and, viii, xxiii

  Christianity and, xiv, xxi, 35, 125

  commands and, xii, xvii, xxiii, xxvi

  conscience and, x–xi

  constitutive motives of, xv

  death and, xiv, xxiv

  divine goodness and, xxiv–xxv

  free will and, x, xii, xviii

practical reason (*cont.*)
  the good and, xiv
  human motives and, xi, xv, xxiv
  human nature and, viii, xii, xv,
    22–24, 35
  human rights and, viii, 7, 128
  is-ought gap and, x, xx–xxiii
  justice and, viii
  law and, 127–28
  liberalism and, xiii
  liberty under law and, xvii
  meaning and, xxiii, xxiv–xxv
  means and ends in, xxi–xxii
  modern political philosophy and,
    ix–x, xii, xx–xxi
  moral judgment and, xv
  natural law and, xxiv, 111, 124–25,
    129
  realism and, 25
  reasons and, xxiii
  rules and, xxiii
  social contract and, viii–ix
  terrorism and, xv–xvi
  theological-political problem of, vii
  value and, xxii
  virtues and, xv, xxii
Prince, The (Machiavelli), x, 35
private and public distinction, 79–80
Protestant Reformation, xi, xx–xxi,
  37–39, 40
Providence, xvii, xxiv, 128–30
prudence, vii, x, xv, xvi–xvii, 39, 88,
  114, 130

rational teleology, xxiii
realism
  human nature and, 24–25
  idealism and, 24–26
  natural law and, 28
  practical reason and, 25
reason. *See* practical reason

relativism, ix
Roman Catholic Church, xiii, 56, 58,
  75, 124, 129
Rousseau, Jean-Jacques, ix, 52–54
Roy, Olivier, 5

same-sex marriage, ix, 16, 17, 123
secularism, vii–viii, 127–28
Seneca, xiv
sex
  denaturalization of, 14–16
  homosexuality and, 14–17 (*see also*
    homosexuality)
  human nature and, 14, 15–16
  law and, 122–23
  replacement by gender of, ix
social construction, 15, 73
social contract, viii–ix, 8, 51–52
Social Contract (Rousseau), 8
Socrates, 54–55
Spinoza, Benedict, xiii, 24, 87, 132n2
  (chap. 2)
state of nature
  consent and, 97
  Hobbes on, viii, xiv, 21–23, 46
  human nature and, 46
  human rights and, 8–9, 46–47, 49,
    51–54, 60–62
  modern political philosophy and, ix,
    xii, xxii, 7–11, 62, 69, 97
  naturalization and denaturalization
    and, 11–16
  natural law and, 7–16
Strauss, Leo, 60
subjectification, 121, 123–24
Summa Theologiae (Aquinas), 129

temperance, vii, xv, 88
terrorism
  human motives and, 104–5
  human nature and, xv–xvi

law and, 103–5
modern political philosophy and,
104–5
natural law and, xv–xvi
practical reason and, xv–xvi
radicalization and, 105
theoretical hypertrophy, xx, xxii,
xxiv–xxv, 24–25
Thomas Aquinas
autonomy and, 67, 135n2
contemporary interpretation of, xvii
freedom and, xviii
God and, 133n26
law and, xvii, 119–20
liberty under law and, xvii
moral responsibility and, xviii
natural law and, xvii, 124, 127, 130
practical reason and, xvii, 125,
128–29
Tocqueville and the Nature of Democracy
(Manent), xx
totalitarianism, xvi, 94, 136n2 (chap. 5)

transgenderism, ix
Treatise on Law (Aquinas), xvii
Trump, Donald, 100

universal guaranteed income, 81–82
universalism, ix, xx, 3–5, 47

virtues
action and, vii
cardinal virtues, vii, xi, xv, xxii, 88
commands and, xxiii, 95–96, 114
desires and, xv
freedom and, 88, 90
human nature and, xv, 103
modern political philosophy and, 44
obeying and, 95–96
old virtues, 90
practical reason and, xv, xxii
role of, vii
terrorism and, xv–xvi
theological virtues, xv
voluntarism, xxiii

PIERRE MANENT is professor emeritus of political philosophy
at the École des Hautes Études en Sciences Sociales. He is the author of numerous books, including *Metamorphoses of the City: On
the Western Dynamic.*

RALPH C. HANCOCK is professor of political science at
Brigham Young University.

DANIEL J. MAHONEY is the Augustinian Boulanger Chair and
professor of political science at Assumption College.

CPSIA information can be obtained
at www.ICGtesting.com
Printed in the USA
LVHW080006180521
687462LV00025B/208